Gillian Gilert

Sage 50
Accounting 2008

For users of Sage 50 Accounts, Sage 50 Accounts Plus, Sage 50
Accounts Professional and the Sage Instant Accounts range

In easy steps is an imprint of Computer Step
Southfield Road · Southam
Warwickshire CV47 0FB · United Kingdom
www.ineasysteps.com

Notice of Liability
Every effort has been made to ensure that this book contains accurate
and current information. However, Computer Step and the author
shall not be liable for any loss or damage suffered by readers as a
result of any information contained herein.

Printed and bound in the United Kingdom

ISBN-13 978-1-84078-354-4
ISBN-10 1-84078-354-0

Contents

5 The Bank 57

6 Products 73

7 Invoices 87

1 Getting Started

This chapter takes you through the stages of preparing Sage 50 for use. It explains initial procedures for setting up Company details and various defaults required by the program.

Introduction

All businesses need accurate accounts, but even with a computer program, if information is not entered correctly, then the accounts could still be wrong. After all, it's easy to blame the computer!

Working through Sage 50 Accounting 2008 in easy steps

This book explains in simple, easy stages how to perform the main tasks required for keeping computerised business accounts. The following chapters show how to:

- Set defaults and Company preferences

- Create customer & supplier records and set up price lists

- Set up opening balances, maintain Bank accounts

- Maintain the Nominal Ledger and run an audit trail

- Generate sales orders and control stock

- Print invoices, credit notes and statements

- Produce history and financial reports

Note: the actual functions available to you will depend on whether you have Sage 50 Accounts, Accounts Plus or Professional. You can even use this book if you work with Sage Instant Accounts.

'Preparing to start' checklist

Before getting started with Sage 50 Accounts 2008, work through the checklist below.

- Check the start date of your company's financial year

- Check with an accountant which VAT scheme is used

- Draw up a list of defaults to use

- Decide on users and passwords

- Backup the data if updating Sage

- Have customer, supplier and bank details to hand

- Product details, recommend a stock take

- A list of all opening balances

Hot tip

Use the demo data provided to fully familiarise yourself with the program before getting started. To do this simply click File, Open from the main menu and select Open Demo Data.

Beware

Some things, once entered, cannot be easily changed. Therefore, make sure you have all the relevant information to hand before using Sage 50 Accounts 2008 for the first time.

Don't forget

It is possible to change the Financial Year start date after you have already commenced using the program.

Starting Sage 50

Turn on your computer and wait for the Windows Desktop to appear. To start your Sage 50 program do the following:

1 Click on the Windows Start button.

2 Click on All Programs – a selection appears

3 Click on the Sage 50 Accounts folder

4 Click on Sage 50 Accounts 2008

5 The Sage 50 desktop appears

Hot tip

Alternatively, if a shortcut has been set up on the Windows desktop, you can open Sage 50 by double-clicking on the shortcut icon:

Beware

Remember that your reporting will not be accurate until all your opening balances have been entered. Ask your accountant for these, if possible before you start using Sage 50.

Hot tip

You can create multiple delivery addresses so that you can have goods delivered to a number of customer sites whilst specifying a different invoice address.

Sage 50 Desktop Views

In Sage 50, the View selector lets you change the display in the Sage desktop work area. Although the options vary from module to module, typically the views may include a List display, a Process Map and a Dashboard.

A Process Map (Customer) is shown on Page 9, whilst the Nominal Ledger List view is shown below. To switch views, simply do the following:

1 Click on Change View

2 Select Company Dashboard

3 The Company Dashboard shows important trading information about your business. Click here to print

Settings

Before Sage 50 can be used there are a number of settings and defaults that need to be entered. The rest of this chapter shows how to do this. When required, select the appropriate settings option from the following list:

 Click on Settings on the Menu bar

 Click on the option required

Hot tip

Click Help on the Sage 50 menu bar, then Shortcut Keys, to bring up a diagram of the available shortcuts. Click on the diagram to close.

11

Using Passwords

The Data Protection Act requires that any system containing confidential information, i.e., financial details etc., should be protected against unauthorised access. Sage 50 uses a password to achieve this. Once you set a password, Sage 50 always prompts you for it at startup.

As with any password, you should avoid writing it down if at all possible. Therefore, try to choose a password that is both easy for you to remember but difficult for someone else to discover. You can decrease the chance of somebody accidentally finding out your password by using a mixture of letters and numbers instead of an actual word.

① From the Settings menu click on Change Password

② Type your password here

③ Repeat the password to confirm

④ Click OK to save password

Hot tip

Try to avoid using obvious things like a name, phone number or car registration as a password. These are far too easy to guess.

Company Preferences

When you run Sage 50 for the first time the Easy Startup Wizard asked for your Company details. Alternatively, after selecting Company Preferences from the settings options, you can enter these details as follows:

1 Enter your company name here

2 Enter your full address details

3 Complete E-Mail & Web addresses

4 Select VAT tab to enter VAT Ref No

5 Click OK to finish

Products and Fixed Assets Categories

After selecting Configuration from the Settings options, you can create different categories for dividing products and fixed assets into for analysis:

1 Select tab & click on the first blank entry

2 Click Edit & enter name

3 Click OK

4 Click Apply button to use

5 Repeat steps 1–4 for Fixed Assets

Setting up & checking Tax Codes

Sage 50 already has the standard UK and EC VAT Rates set for you together with the code T1 (standard rate – currently 17.5%) set as the default tax code. Here is a list of the codes automatically set up during installation:

T0   –   zero rated transactions

T1   –   standard rate

T2   –   exempt transactions

T4   –   sales to customers in EC*

T7   –   zero rated purchases from suppliers in EC*

T8   –   standard rated purchases from suppliers in EC*

T9   –   transactions not involving VAT

(* Outside the UK)

There are 100 VAT codes available in Sage 50. To enter or change VAT tax rates, use Configuration from the settings options:

1   Click Tax Codes tab & required code

2   Click Edit

3   Enter percentage rate

4   Tick if VAT rate is for an EC Code

5   Enter Description & click OK

6   Click Apply to use

Beware

It is important to use the correct VAT codes. If you are unsure of the current UK or EU VAT Tax rates then contact HM Revenue & Customs.

Don't forget

T1 is the standard UK VAT rate code.

13

Hot tip

Sage 50 uses T9 as the default tax code for all the routines that are non-vatable, e.g. journal entries error corrections and Bank.

...cont'd

Financial Year

The start of the financial year is entered during the installation of Sage 50 or before entering any transactions, but it is also possible to change it later:

1 From Settings on the menu bar click on Financial Year

2 To change year select the Change button

3 Click Yes in the next two prompt windows, select year and click OK

Account Status

A handy feature within Sage 50 is that you can assign an account status to each of your accounts. You can add an account status at any time to the ten already set up via the Configuration Editor:

1 Click on the Account Status tab & highlight a blank line

2 Click Edit

3 Enter the Status Name

4 Tick if you want this status to place accounts 'on hold'

5 Click OK, then Apply to use

Currency & the Euro

Sage 50 is already set up with the currencies of the EC countries, but not the exchange rates. These details can be edited or other countries set up as required:

1 Click on Settings, Currencies and highlight the currency you want to edit or select the first blank record to enter a new currency

Number	Name	Code	Symbol	Exchange Rate
1	Pound Sterling	GBP	£	BASE
2	US Dollar	USD	$	0.000000
3	Euro	EUR	€	0.000000
4	Argentinean Peso	ARS	$	0.000000
5	Australian Dollar	AUD	$	0.000000
6	Brazilian Real	BRL	$	0.000000
7	Canadian Dollar	CAD	$	0.000000

US Dollar
Exchange rate: 0.000000 US Dollar per Pound Sterling
Reverse: 0.000000 Pound Sterling per US Dollar
Currency units: dollars and cents

[Edit]   [Close]

2 Click Edit to bring up the Edit Currency box

3 Enter the name of the Currency

4 Complete the Currency Code & the Currency symbol

5 Enter the Currency exchange rate

Edit Currency
Currency Details
Currency name: US Dollar
Currency Code: USD   Currency symbol: $
Exchange Rate
0.000000 US Dollar per Pound Sterling
0.000000 Pound Sterling per US Dollar
Currency Units
Major currency unit: dollars
Minor currency unit: cents
[OK] [Cancel]

6 Enter the Major & Minor currency units

7 Click OK, then Close the Currencies box

Hot tip

Simply press F5 to access the Euro Calculator in any numeric field that displays the calculator button icon.

Hot tip

The calculator can be used to either view an amount converted from Sterling to a Euro/Foreign Currency or to convert a Euro/Foreign Currency amount to Sterling.

Beware

Exchange rates change frequently, so make sure you have the latest rates entered before recording a foreign currency transaction. Up to date rates are available from a number of sources, including the Internet (e.g. www.xe.com).

Customer & Supplier Defaults

When creating a new customer or supplier, details about credit limit, terms, discount etc. are needed. Customer and Supplier records are discussed in Chapters Two & Three respectively but before this, defaults need to be set up.

Hot tip

For customers, default nominal codes (N/C) start at 4000.

1 Select Customer Defaults from the Settings options

2 Enter defaults for your customer records on the first Tab

3 Click on the relevant Tabs to enter Statements, Ageing Balance and appropriate Discount defaults

Don't forget

A customer can be a member of a price list. However, as a customer can only belong to one price list, if you want to change the list that the selected customer belongs to, select the price list you require from the drop-down list. Note that on each price list, additional discounts can still be applied.

4 Click OK to save the Customer Defaults entered

5 Now select Supplier Defaults from the Settings options

6 Enter relevant Supplier Defaults

7 Use Ageing Tab to enter Aged Balances Period, specifying calendar months or days

Hot tip

Default nominal codes for suppliers start at 5000.

8 Click OK to save Supplier Defaults

Product Defaults

Defaults also need to be set up for Products:

1. Select Product Defaults from the Settings options

2. Enter the Nominal Account code here

3. Allocate the correct Tax Code for the Product

4. Complete the rest of the defaults as necessary

5. Enter the Decimal Point placing for the product

6. Click OK to save this information

Product Defaults

Details | Descriptions

Defaults

Sales Nominal Code	4000
Tax Code	T1 17.50
Purchase Nominal Code	
Unit of Sale	Each
Category	1 Paper Products
Department	007
Image Options	Maintain Image Size

Decimal Precision

Quantity D.P.	2
Unit D.P.	2

OK   Cancel

Hot tip

Use the Finder button on the right of the Nominal Code box to speed up code entry.

Control Accounts

Sage 50 uses Control Accounts to make automatic double-entry postings to the ledger.

1. To view or edit these Nominal Codes select Control Accounts from the Settings options

2. To change a Control account click on the nominal code and type the new code or use the Finder button

3. Click OK to save and close or Cancel to abandon changes

Control Accounts

Control Account	N/C
Debtors Control	1100
Creditors Control	2100
Default Bank	1200
VAT on Sales	2200
VAT on Purchases	2201
Sales Discount	4009
Purchase Discount	5009
Retained Earnings	3200
Default Sales	4000
Accruals	2109
Prepayments	1103
Bad Debts	8100
Mispostings	9999
Suspense	9998

OK   Cancel

Beware

Unless you have created your own Chart of Accounts, the Control accounts should never need changing.

Finance Rates

Finance rates need to be set up before any credit charges can be applied to your customers.

Hot tip

When a Finance Charge Rate is applied to a transaction, the first rate charged will be applied monthly until the invoice is paid.

1 Select Configuration from the Settings menu and click on the Terms tab to bring up the Finance Charge Rates box

2 Click on Add to enter a new finance rate charge

Don't forget

You must first have set up your finance rates and the date from which they are to be applied before you can use the Charges option on the Customer toolbar.

3 Enter the date the charge is to be applied from

4 Enter the Base Rate as a percentage

5 Enter an additional charge if applicable

Hot tip

Use the Delete button on the Finance Charge Rates window to remove any unwanted charges.

6 Click OK to save new finance rate or Cancel to return to the Finance Charge Rates box

Set Finance Charge Rate

Date Applying From	06/04/2008
Base Rate %	4.50
Additional %	0.00

OK   Cancel

7 Click Close to finish

18

2 The Customer Ledger

Learn how to use the Customer (Sales) Ledger to maintain customer records and create new ones as well as enter credit notes and invoices. See how to view transaction activity, set up a customer price list, produce an overdue payments letter, apply credit charges and mark an invoice as disputed.

Keeping a Financial System

It is essential for all businesses to have a system to record and monitor their business and financial transactions. This information needs to be accurately recorded and kept up to date if it is to present a true financial position.

Such a system will involve the recording of transactions using the traditional method of bookkeeping or advanced accounting procedures, where financial reports (i.e. profit & loss statements and balance sheet, etc.) can be produced.

These reports provide the Management with information on sales, purchases, turnover, expenses, debtors and creditors, assets and liabilities, and more importantly, if the business has made a profit.

HM Revenue and Customs will also need accurate accounts, which must conform to general bookkeeping and accounting procedures. This is vital for Tax & VAT Returns. Visit the website at www.hmrc.gov.uk for up to date information on online filing and payments.

This information is also of importance to your Bank Manager, especially if there is a need to borrow money to ease cash flow problems or help set up a new business venture. Likewise, potential investors in your business may first want to see the true financial position of your accounts before making a decision.

Computerised systems have now removed the majority of time consuming and repetitive tasks of manual accounting. Businesses can check their financial status on a daily basis, or over a designated period of time. This valuable information will aid important decision making and business planning and is crucial for forecasting whether a business will succeed or fail.

Sage 50 makes keeping computerised accounts easy. Many of the report templates needed are provided with the package, so producing accurate business reports is a simple matter, provided, of course, that all information has been entered correctly. The following chapters guide you through the processes involved in keeping accurate and up to date computerised financial accounts for your business.

The Customers Toolbar

The Customers toolbar provides features for creating customer records and viewing transaction activity, producing invoices and credit notes, marking invoices as disputed and applying credit charges. Customer Statements are produced here, plus letters, a range of reports and generating price lists.

New
Creates a new Customer Account

Record
Opens a Customer Record

Price List
To set up a Customer Price List

Activity
Opens Customer Activity

Aged
Opens Customer Aged Balances

Invoice
Opens the Batch Customer Invoices window

Credit
Opens the Batch Customer Credits window

Dispute
Opens the Disputed Items window

Charges
Opens the Credit Charges window

Phone
To automatically Dial a Customer

Labels
To print Customer Labels

Letters
To print Standard Letters to Customers

Statement
To print Customer Statements

Reports
To run Customer Reports

Creating Customer Records

In this window, a customer record can be added, edited or deleted. You can record agreed credit terms and even log any contact you have with a customer, such as telephone calls and who you spoke to. You can now also record if invoices are sent electronically.

1 Select Customers from the Sage 50 navigation bar

2 Click on Record to bring up the Customer Record window

3 Use Details tab to store basic customer information

4 Use the O/B button if an opening Balance is required

5 Tick here if invoices are sent electronically

6 Use the Credit Control tab to enter any credit terms you have agreed for this customer

7 Click Save to store the Customer Record

8 Enter a new record or click Close to finish

Viewing transactions

Once customer activity has taken place, Sage 50 offers you a variety of options for checking customer transaction details:

- View customer invoices, receipts, credit notes and balances on a monthly basis, as a graph or table

- Use the Activity option to see a breakdown of each customer's transactions

- View or print the Customer's aged balances

1 Click on the Activity tab in the Customer Record window

2 Select a transaction, all items appear in the lower pane

3 Use the scroll bar to move through all the transactions

4 Click on Show to select another range of transactions, enter dates if choosing Custom Range then click OK

Don't forget

Note that the following codes indicate the transaction type:

SI = Sales Invoice
SR = Sales Receipt
SC = Sales Credit Note
SD = Sales Discount
SA = Sales Receipt on Account

23

Hot tip

Use the Orders tab to quickly view a history of the sales orders a customer has placed with you. Simply double click on an order in the list to bring up the sales order record.

5 Select Close to return to Customer window

Price List

In Sage 50, different price lists can be set up and customers allocated to the price list of your choice. For each Price List products can be added and different prices set up accordingly. For example, you can create custom lists for Trade, Retail, Summer or Winter Sales and Special Offers.

To create a new Price List do the following:

Hot tip

Where a selected customer is already on another price list, Sage 50 asks if you want to transfer this customer to the new list. Click Yes to transfer the customer to the new list or Yes to All to transfer all customers already on another list to the new list.

1 From the Customers toolbar click on the Price List button to bring up the Price Lists box

2 Click New to open the New Price List window

3 Enter Reference and Name

4 Click Save

Hot tip

To add more than one customer at a time to your list, simply hold down the Control key and click on your selection during Step 6.

5 Select Customers tab & click Add to bring up a list

6 Select Customer

7 Click OK

8 Click Save, then Close and Close again

Batch Customer Invoice

Invoices are important business transaction documents and record detailed information about the goods or services supplied to the customer. Briefly, these details include the invoice number, name and address of the customer, date of sale, details of goods and or services supplied, details of discount, total amount of money due and terms of trade.

There are different types of invoices and Chapter Seven shows you how to create a product or a service invoice, as well as automatically creating an invoice from a sales order. However, any invoices produced manually (Batch Invoices) and sent to customers also need recording. No printout is produced.

To record a batch customer invoice do the following:

1 Choose Invoice from the Customers toolbar

2 Enter the customer Account Code or use the finder button to display a list of codes

3 Change invoice date if different from current system date

4 Enter the Invoice Number and a Ref. Number, as required

5 Change Nominal Code or Department if different

6 Enter Net value of invoice

7 Click Save to update the nominal ledger and customer details (details posted), then Close

Hot tip

Where you only know the gross value of an invoice, enter it in the Net box and use the Calc. Net button (or press the F9 shortcut key) to let Sage 50 work out the correct Net value and VAT due.

Hot tip

For a list of useful data entry Shortcut Keys see the inside front cover at the start of this book.

Beware

Always check that the correct Tax Code is used. See page 13.

Batch Customer Credit Note

A credit note is used, for example, where an error is made and a customer has been overcharged on an invoice. Sometimes, damaged goods are returned and so a credit note is issued showing the amount due to the customer.

Like batch invoicing, credit notes processed manually need to be entered. To record batch credit notes:

Hot tip

To check the credit note has been posted, make a note of the balance for the appropriate customer in the Customers window before entering the credit note, then check that the balance has reduced by the correct amount after performing Step 6.

1 Click Credit from the Customers toolbar to bring up the Batch Customer Credits window

2 Enter the customer Account Code

3 The screen displays the defaults for the nominal account code posting, VAT rate to be applied & department

| A/C | Business Exhibitions | | | | | | | Tax Rate | 17.50 |
| N/C | Sales North | | | | | | | Total | 0.00 |

A/C	Date	Credit No	Ex.Ref	N/C	Dept	Project Ref	Details	Net	T/C	VAT
BUS001	20/12/2007			4000	001			0.00	T1	0.00
								0.00		0.00

Save | Discard | Calc. Net | Memorise | Recall | Close

Don't forget

When looking at Customer activity, the transaction type (Tp) code SC indicates a Sales Credit Note.

4 Enter credit details for each customer in the same way as for batch invoice

5 Check all values are correct & click Save to post the details or Discard to start again

6 Click Close to return to the Customers window

Debtors Analysis

To identify debtors and monitor cashflow, customers' outstanding balances and transactions need to be regularly checked. These transactions are grouped by the age of the debt, either on calendar months or based on a period of days, e.g. 30, 60 and 90 days etc. Debt chasing letters can be issued if required. A business may use this information to calculate interest charges for late payment.

1 From the Customers window select the required customer

2 Click Aged to bring up the Aged Balances Date Defaults box

Aged Balances Date Defaults

Enter Range

Aged Balance Report Date   13/07/2008

Include Payments Up To   13/07/2008

OK   Cancel

3 Enter the date to be used for calculating the aged balances

4 Enter the date to include payments up to

5 Click OK to bring up the Aged Balances window

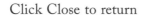

6 To see a graph format click the Graph tab

7 For a transaction breakdown click on Detailed

8 Click Close to return

Hot tip

From the Settings menu select Customer Defaults, then the Ageing tab to change the age of the debt from calendar months to period of days, or vice versa.

27

Beware

When you select the required customers in the Customers window, always check that the dates in the Aged Balance Report Date and the Include Payments Up To boxes cover those selected customers.

Credit Charges

A payment which is 30 days overdue is regarded, by default, as late. If you need to change payment terms, do the following:

1 From the navigation bar choose the Customers button

2 Highlight the appropriate customer or customers, then click the Record button

3 Click on the Credit Control tab to bring up the Credit Control details box

---

Hot tip

Use the Memo box to keep notes on any credit agreement you may have negotiated with the selected customer.

Hot tip

To apply charges to customers whose payments are overdue simply click Charges from the Customers window to run the Credit Charges Wizard.

Customer - ABS Garages Ltd

Details | Defaults | Credit Control | Sales | Orders | Projects | Graphs | Activity | Bank | Contacts | Memo

Terms

Credit Limit	4000.00
Settlement Due	30 Days
Sett.Discount	2.50
Payment Due	30
Average Time to Pay	0 Days
Trading Terms Text	30 Days
Credit Ref.	TS3812
Bureau	Trade Safe
Credit Position	Good
Account status	0 Open
DUNS Number	

Credit Review

A/C Opened	13/12/2005
Last Credit Review	09/09/2007
Next Credit Review	09/09/2008
Application Date	10/12/2004
Date Received	11/12/2004

Memo:

A/C open date:
Trade references checked out ok.
Passed credit check review account 3-12 months

First Review
Satisfactory account

Restrictions

☑ Can charge credit ☐ Restrict mailing
☑ Terms agreed ☐ Account On Hold

Save | Discard | Delete | Previous | Next | Print List | New Order | New Invoice | New Project | Close

---

4 Enter new details in Payment Due

5 Apply account restrictions here if desired, such as placing account on hold or allowing credit to be charged

6 Change any of the other terms as required, then click Save

7 Click Close to return to the Customers window, then Close again

---

Beware

Before you can use the Credit Charges Wizard, finance rates must have first been set up.

Disputed Invoices

There may be times when an invoice is questioned by the customer, so until an agreement is made the invoice can be marked as disputed. This option also applies to any invoices not fully paid. Once the problem is resolved, you can remove the disputed flag (indicator). To mark an invoice as disputed:

1 Click on the Dispute button in the Customers window to bring up the Disputed Items window

2 Enter the Customer Account Code and press the Tab key

3 Click on the transaction you want to mark as disputed

Don't forget

Don't forget to first set up Dispute Reasons using the Configuration Editor. This will then give you more accurate reporting when you need to check why an item has been marked as disputed in the future.

Disputed Items

A/C `BUS001`   Name `Business Exhibitions`

No	Type	Date	Ref	Details	T/C	Amount	Dis	Dispute Reason
1299	SI	30/03/2008	49	PC Combo Pack 3	T1	1546.59		
1300	SI	30/03/2008	49	SIMM 32mb 100Mhz	T1	154.67		
1301	SI	30/03/2008	49	Copy Paper - Standard Gr...	T1	178.72		
1302	SI	30/03/2008	49	JP010 Jet Printer	T1	144.35		
1303	SI	30/03/2008	49	Rubber Bands - Selection ...	T1	12.37		
1304	SI	30/03/2008	49	JP030 Jet Printer Cartridge	T1	129.92		
1307	SI	05/04/2008	74	Whiteboard Drywipe (100...	T1	4576.69		

[Save] [Discard] [Dispute]   [Close]

Hot tip

To remove the Dispute status of an invoice simply highlight it and click on the Dispute button again.

29

4 Click Dispute

Details
Select a reason to explain why this item is being disputed.
Reason code `2 - Wrong Item`
[OK] [Cancel]

5 Select Reason & Click OK

6 Note that transaction is now marked as 'd'

7 Click Save to record the transaction

8 Click Close to return to the Customers window, then Close again

Don't forget

Remember that if you are using Standard VAT, invoices marked as disputed are still included in the VAT Return.

Customer Reports & Modem

Sage 50 provides you with a wide range of ready-designed customer reports to suit the majority of needs. To print or view a customer report, do the following:

 Click on the Reports button in the Customers window

 Click here on the appropriate folder & select the report you require from the list

 Select output, i.e. Preview, then click Generate Report

 After printing Close each window

Modem

For some features, you need to have a modem fitted in your PC. By default, the F11 key is set up by Sage 50 to open the Control Panel so that you can check if your computer has a modem installed, as follows:

 Press the F11 key to bring up the Windows Control Panel

 Double-click on the Phone and Modem icon

 Click the Modems tab to see if a modem is fitted

Customer Letters and Labels

Occasionally, you may have a need to send standard information to a customer, such as change of address, or to chase up an overdue payment. All of the necessary information needed for these letters is taken from your records.

A number of the more common standard letters are provided with Sage 50, but alternatively there is the option to create new ones. The new letters can be stored for future use.

1. From the Customers window, select the customer or customers you want to send a letter to

2. Click the Letters button on the Customers toolbar to bring up the Customer Letters list

3. Click on the letter required

4. Ensure Preview is checked

5. Click Generate Report to produce the report

6. If correct, click Print, then OK

7. Click here to Close

Beware

To produce labels for all your customers in one go simply click the Clear button before pressing the Labels button on the Customers toolbar.

The Customer Statement

To keep customers up to date about their financial position, customer statements should be sent out on a regular basis, normally once a month. The statement shows details of all recorded customer transactions, together with a balance figure.

Don't forget

You can also use the Customer Statement window to delete statements no longer required, or to modify and design your own.

1 From the Customers window click on the Statements button to bring up the Customer Statements window

2 Choose the statement layout you require

3 Ensure Preview is checked

4 Click Generate Report to bring up the selection Criteria box

Hot tip

To preview a sample report, simply enter a small number of records in the box provided.

5 Enter Customer Reference range

6 Enter Transaction Date From & To

7 Click OK to preview the statement

8 Use the Zoom button on the preview to zoom in or out if you need to check any statement detail

9 Click Print to print the statement, then Close all windows

3 The Supplier Ledger

See how to create and maintain supplier records within the Supplier (Purchase) Ledger. You will learn how to view details of invoices received and payments made to suppliers using graphs and reports.

The Supplier Toolbar

The Supplier toolbar has many similar buttons to the Customer toolbar, and again provides you with facilities for setting up records, checking supplier activity, recording invoices, credit notes and reporting.

 New Creates a new Supplier Record

 Record Opens a Supplier Record

 Price List To set up a Supplier Price List

 Activity View Supplier Activity

 Aged View Supplier Aged Balances

 Invoice Record Supplier Invoices

 Credit Record Supplier Credit Notes

 Dispute Opens the Disputed Items window

 Phone To Automatically Dial a Supplier

 Labels To Print Supplier Labels

 Letters To Print Standard Letters to Suppliers

 Reports To Run Supplier Reports

Creating Supplier Records

Within this window you can view, edit or delete a supplier record. A new supplier record can also be added if you have all of the details to hand. To add a new supplier first select Suppliers from the Sage 50 toolbar, then do the following:

 1 Select Suppliers from the Sage 50 navigation bar

2 Click on Record to bring up the Supplier Record window

3 Use Details tab to store basic supplier information

4 Use the O/B button if an opening Balance is required

5 Tick here if orders are sent electronically

6 Enter credit terms using the Credit Control tab & the Bank tab to record bank details for payment transfers

7 Click Save to store the Supplier Record

8 Enter a new record or click Close to finish

Using Search

The Search function available within the suppliers window can help save you valuable time when searching for specific information regarding supplier transactions. The following example shows you how to produce a list of suppliers you owe money to:

Hot tip

This useful Search feature is also available within other program windows, such as Customers, Products, Nominal, Financials and Invoicing.

1 Click the Search button in the bottom left hand corner of the Suppliers window to bring up the Search window

2 Click Where in the first column

3 Select Balance in this field

Search -				
Only select records from 'Suppliers'				
Join	Field		Condition	Value
Where	Balance		Is Greater Than	0.00
	Account Type Member			
	Average Time To Pay			
	Balance			
	Balance Current			
	Balance Future			

Expression:
Where 'Balance' > '0.00'

[Wizard] [Discard] [Open] [Save] [Save As]   [Apply] [Close]

Hot tip

To search using part information, select the Is Equal To condition and preceed the Value with the symbol $. For example, use $W1 and the field Account Address Line 5 to search for all Suppliers in the London W1 area.

4 Select Is Greater Than in the Condition column

5 Enter zero in the Value field

6 Click Apply & Close to return to the Suppliers window

7 Note that only records matching the search are displayed. The title bar indicates the Search is applied

8 To cancel the search and show all records, click this icon

Suppliers　　　　　　　(10 of 16 Records matched)　Change View ▼　✕

Supplier Activity

This feature enables you to view each supplier's transactions in detail. If less complete information is required, you can define a transaction or date range to limit the view:

 1 From the Suppliers window select the supplier you want to look at, then click on Activity

2 Select a transaction, all items appear in the lower pane

3 Use the scroll bar to move through all the transactions

4 Click on Show to select another range of transactions

5 Click Close to return to the Suppliers window

Hot tip

To view this screen from the Supplier Record window, enter the A/C for the supplier required (if none selected) then click on the Activity tab.

Hot tip

Double-click on any Purchase Invoice (PI) transaction to bring up the relevant Product Purchase Order.

37

Don't forget

Note that the following codes indicate the transaction type:

PI = Purchase Invoice
PP = Purchase Payment
PC = Purchase Credit Note
PD = Discount on a Purchase Payment
PA = Purchase Payment on Account

Supplier Aged Balance

Aged balance is the term given to the time lapse of outstanding debt, whether owed to you or by you. Sage 50 lets you view the amount of money you owe your Suppliers, grouped on the age of the debt. It is common practice for businesses to give 30 days credit, but other terms are sometimes negotiated. Sage 50 default aged periods are 30, 60 and 90 days.

Don't forget

The age period is set through Supplier Defaults from the Settings menu. You can base it on either calendar months or a period of days, specified by you. Remember also that ageing is relative to the program date.

1 From the Suppliers window, click on the supplier you require (or ensure none selected to view all) and select the Aged button from the toolbar

2 Enter dates and click OK to display the Aged Balances Report

Aged Balances Date Defaults	
Enter Range	
Aged Balance Report Date	12/07/2008
Include Payments Up To	01/07/2008

OK   Cancel

Hot tip

If you need to enter a date only a few days either side of that displayed simply use the cursor up or down keys on the keyboard.

Aged Balances as of 12th July 2008

Aged Balances | Graph

A/C	YTD	Credit Limit	Balance	Future	Current	1 Month(s)	2 Month(s)	3 Month(s)	(
CON001	0.00	17000.00	1644.39						164
HIG002	0.00	1000.00							
MCN001	0.00	10000.00	24734.12						2473
MEA001	0.00	0.00							
NEW001	0.00	10000.00							
QUA001	0.00	20000.00	30.22						3
SDE001	0.00	5000.00	352.50						35
STU001	0.00	4500.00							
SUP001	2926.80	15000.00	9164.95		3426.20				573
SUP002	0.00	3000.00	1762.50						178
THO001	0.00	4000.00	337.11						33

Future	Current	1 Month(s)	2 Month(s)	3 Month(s)	Older	Balance	Creditors
0.00	3426.20	0.00	0.00	0.00	41076.48	44502.68	44502.68

Detailed   Print List   Close

3 To see the transactions which make up the aged balance click Detailed

4 Close each window when finished

Recording Supplier Invoices

Invoices received from your suppliers can be entered a few at a time using the Batch Supplier Invoices window. You have full flexibility using this option, such as posting each invoice item to a different nominal account if need be, or allocating to a different VAT code, such as from default VAT to zero VAT. To enter invoices, do the following:

1 From the Suppliers window click Invoice to bring up the Batch Supplier Invoices window

2 Type the supplier's account code or use the Finder button

3 Enter the Date and other invoice details, amending the Nominal (N/C) and Tax (T/C) codes if necessary

4 When all details are correct and all invoices have been entered, click Save to post the details then click Close to return to the Suppliers window

5 Note that the Supplier's record now displays the new balance, then click Close again

39

Beware

Always check that the correct tax code has been selected for the VAT to avoid errors later. Sage 50 enters T1 (standard rate) for you by default. You may need to change this to T0 for transactions which are zero rated or to T9 for any not involving VAT.

Don't forget

Remember that with batch invoices, no printouts are generated of the transaction entered. Use activity reports if you require a paper copy.

Don't forget

'Posting' means updating the Nominal ledger and relevant supplier's details. If you do not wish to save this batch, choose the Discard button to clear the data and start again.

Supplier Credit Notes

Occasionally, goods ordered from suppliers may arrive damaged or incomplete. The supplier issues you a credit note reducing the amount owed. Credit notes are recorded using the Credit option from the Suppliers window.

If a credit note contains a number of items, for your benefit it is advisable to enter each transaction individually, but giving them the same account code, date and reference. Sage 50 groups these together and lists them as a single credit note. You can then view the note in more detail using Activity from the Suppliers window.

1. From the Suppliers window click Credit

2. Enter the supplier Account Code. Use the Finder button if you don't have the code

3. Enter the credit note Date and remaining details

Don't forget

It is always advisable to check the changes you have made by noting the before and after outstanding balance. This will save time later if a mistake has been made.

4. Click Save to update the nominal ledger & record the credit details, then Close to return to the Suppliers window

5. Note that the Balance has changed, then click Close

Hot tip

It is useful to enter the invoice number that the credit note refers to in the Reference (Ex.Ref) box for identification. This will appear in the details under Financials.

Supplier Letters and Labels

As with Customers, Sage 50 includes the facility to produce preformatted letters and labels for your suppliers. You can create whatever standard letters or label layouts you wish. All necessary address information etc. is taken from the stored supplier details.

To produce the standard letter informing suppliers of your change of address, do the following:

1 From the Suppliers window click Letters to bring up the Supplier Letters window

2 Click on the letter required and ensure Preview is selected

3 Click Generate Report to produce the report

4 Check the letters and click Print, then OK

Hot tip

The Credit Control tab window has an option to Restrict mailing. Use this to control who you send mailshots to.

5 When finished, Close all windows

Beware

Always remember to check that the correct paper, labels and printer type have been selected before printing to avoid wasting time and paper.

Labels

To produce address labels for your suppliers, click the Labels button from the Suppliers window then carry out Steps 2–5 as above.

Supplier Reports

You can generate a wide range of detailed reports on your suppliers. These reports are produced from the information you entered about suppliers and their transactions. Sage 50 already has a considerable number of reports set up, but if any further reports are required you can create them using the Report Designer (see Chapter Twelve). To run or view a supplier report:

1 Click on the Reports button in the Suppliers window

2 Click here on the required folder and select a report

Supplier Reports	
Description	**File Name**
⊟ 🗁 Aged Creditors Reports	
🗁 Aged Creditors Analysis (Contacts)	SPLAGEC.report
🗁 Aged Creditors Analysis (Contacts) - By Balance (Desc...	PL_Agecb.report
🗁 Aged Creditors Analysis (Contacts) - By Balance (Desc...	PL_Agcbd.report
🗁 Aged Creditors Analysis (Contacts) with Disputed Items	Splagecd.report
🗁 Aged Creditors Analysis (Contacts) with Foreign Values	SPLAGECF.report
🗁 Aged Creditors Analysis (Detailed)	SPLAGED.report
🗁 Aged Creditors Analysis (Detailed) - By Balance (Desc...	PL_Agedb.report
🗁 Aged Creditors Analysis (Detailed) - By Balance (Desc...	PL_Agdbd.report
🗁 Aged Creditors Analysis (Detailed) with Disputed Items	Splagedd.report
🗁 Aged Creditors Analysis (Detailed) with Foreign Values	SPLAGEFD.report
🗁 Aged Creditors Analysis (Detailed) with Foreign Values ...	Splagefd.report
🗁 Aged Creditors Analysis (Summary)	SPLAGES.report
🗁 Aged Creditors Analysis (Summary) - By Balance (Desc...	PL_Agesb.report
🗁 Aged Creditors Analysis (Summary) - By Balance (Desc...	PL_Agsbd.report

Generate Report | Preview

New | Edit | Delete | Expand | Tidy | Close

3 Select Printer or Preview

4 Click Generate Report to produce report

5 If a Criteria box appears, enter the From and To details, then click OK

Criteria	
Criteria Values	
Enter the values to use for the criteria in this report	
Supplier Ref	Between (Inclusive) ▾	and ZZZZZZZZ
Transaction Date	Between (Inclusive) ▾ 01/01/1980	and 11/10/2008
Inc Future Tran	☐	
Exc Later Payments	☐	
Preview a sample report for a specified number of records or transactions (0 for all) 0	
Help	OK Cancel

6 After printing, Close all windows

4 The Nominal Ledger

This chapter explains the important role played by the Nominal Ledger and how its accounts detail the flow of money in and out of the business. You will be shown how to analyse these account transactions using graphs and activity reports.

The Nominal Toolbar

The Nominal toolbar buttons provide you with facilities for setting up records, viewing account activity, making journal entries, setting up prepayments and accruals, working on the chart of accounts and reporting.

 New   Creates a new Nominal Account

 Record   Opens a Nominal Record

 Activity   View a Nominal Account's Activity

 Journals   Enter Journal double-entries

 Reversals   Process Nominal Ledger Reversals

 Prepay   Enter Nominal Ledger Prepayments

 Accrual   Enter Nominal Ledger Accrual

 COA   Opens the Chart of Accounts

 Reports   To Run Nominal Ledger Report

The Nominal Ledger

The Nominal Ledger, also referred to as the General Ledger, is a grouped analysis of your sales and purchase transactions. For example, when a sales or purchase invoice is posted to the sales or purchase ledger, Sage 50 records it in the Nominal Ledger against the appropriate Nominal account number.

It therefore contains all the accounts for your business, e.g. sales, purchases, expenses, VAT, cash and bank, sundry income, fixed assets, liabilities, capital and owner's drawings. However, it does not keep details of debtors and creditors. These are held in the respective sales and purchase ledgers.

The Nominal accounts let you see quickly where your money is. Information from here is used in the production of management reports to tell you how your business is performing.

1 Click Modules from the menu bar, then Nominal Ledger

2 Select the Ledger view you prefer from these options

Nominal Ledger

N/C	Name	Debit	
0010	Freehold Property		
0011	Leasehold Property		
0020	Plant and Machinery	50000.00	
0021	Plant/Machinery Depreciation		
0030	Office Equipment		
0031	Office Equipment Depreciation		
0040	Furniture and Fixtures	16900.00	
0041	Furniture/Fixture Depreciation		93.00
0050	Motor Vehicles	20300.00	
0051	Motor Vehicles Depreciation		2091.92
1001	Stock	35000.00	
1002	Work in Progress		
1003	Finished Goods		
1100	Debtors Control Account	85714.54	
1101	Sundry Debtors		
1102	Other Debtors		
1103	Prepayments		
1200	Bank Current Account		5290.69

0 of 148 accounts selected, total   Debit   0.00   Credit   0.00

[Search] [Swap] [Clear] [Delete] [Print List] [Expand All] [Collapse All] [Send] [Duplicate] [Close]

3 Click Close when finished

In Sage 50, you can choose a standard set of nominal accounts during installation, unless in the Startup Wizard you decided to create your own nominal structure. Note that the latter option only creates the Control Accounts for you.

Don't forget

To help you work with the Nominal Ledger, here is some of the standard nominal accounts used by Sage 50:

- Asset Accounts from 0001 to 1999
- Liability Accounts from 2000 to 3999
- Income Accounts from 4000 to 4999
- Purchase Accounts from 5000 to 5999
- Direct Expenses from 6000 to 6999
- Overheads from 7000 to 9999

45

Hot tip

A shortcut for bringing up the Nominal Ledger window is to click on the following button in the Sage 50 navigation bar:

Nominal Records

You can tailor the nominal accounts to exactly meet your needs by using the Nominal Record window. You have the facility to add, edit and delete nominal accounts as well as viewing transactions posted to each account on a monthly basis.

Using the Record window you can also set budget values for each month of your financial year for a particular nominal account. You can also compare the actual monthly figures against the budget values to keep track of how close you are to meeting targets. To add a nominal account record, do the following:

1 Click Record from the Nominal Ledger to bring up the Nominal Record window

Nominal Record - Sales - North West

Details | Graphs | Activity | Memo

N/C: 4005 — New Account
Name: Sales - North West
Balance: 0.00 — Account Type: Nominal Account

Month	Actuals	Budgets	To end Mar 2008
B/F	0.00	0.00	0.00
Apr	0.00	7000.00	6000.00 Dr
May	0.00	6800.00	0.00
Jun	0.00	3200.00	0.00
Jul	0.00	5200.00	0.00
Aug	0.00	3500.00	0.00
Sep	0.00	3500.00	0.00
Oct	0.00	5500.00	0.00
Nov	0.00	6300.00	0.00
Dec	0.00	3800.00	0.00
Jan	0.00	5000.00	0.00
Feb	0.00	7000.00	0.00
Mar	0.00	7500.00	0.00
Future	0.00	0.00	0.00
Total	0.00	64300.00	6000.00 Dr

Save | Discard | Delete | Previous | Next | Print List | Close

2 In the Details tab box, enter a new nominal account code

3 Press the Tab key and note that this is a New Account

4 Enter new account Name, Budget and Prior Year values

5 Click Save to store details or Discard to start again

Viewing Nominal Transactions

You can view your Nominal Ledger transactions by using:

- Graphs
- Activity reports
- Table formats

Transaction Analysis using Graphs

A range of 2D and 3D charts is available in Sage 50 to visually compare your current year's trading against the previous year and any budgets you have put in place.

1 From the Nominal Ledger window, select the nominal account you wish to view

2 Click Record, then select the Graphs tab to display data in graphical form

3 To choose a different type of graph, click here, then click on the graph required

4 Click on the Printer button to print out the graph

5 Click Close to return to the Nominal Ledger window

...cont'd

Viewing Nominal Account Activity

You will occasionally need to view transactions that have been posted to the nominal ledger accounts. To do this from the Nominal Ledger window:

1 From the Nominal Ledger window click on the nominal account you wish to view

2 Click on the toolbar Activity button to bring up the Activity window

3 Select a transaction, all items appear in the lower pane

4 Use the scroll bar to move through all the transactions

5 Click on Show to select another range of transactions

6 Use Previous & Next buttons to view other nominal accounts, if more than one selected in Step 1

7 Click Close to return to the Nominal Ledger

Don't forget

Transactions already cleared from the audit trail are shown as one carried forward total and displayed as an Opening Balance (O/BAL).

Don't forget

Each line of the Activity list box represents a single invoice, credit note, payment on account or receipt.

Hot tip

You can select more than one account to view at a time. Simply use the Next and Previous buttons to scroll through them.

Transaction Codes

Transactions in the Activity window are indicated by a type (Tp) or transaction code, allocated by Sage 50 as follows:

BR (Bank Receipt)	SD (Discount on Sales Receipt)
BP (Bank Payment)	SA (Sales Receipt on Account)
CP (Cash Payment)	PI (Purchase Invoice)
CR (Cash Receipt)	PP (Purchase Payment)
JD (Journal Debit)	PC (Purchase Credit)
JC (Journal Credit)	PD (Discount on Purchase Payment)
SI (Sales Invoice)	PA (Purchase Payment on Account)
SR (Sales Receipt)	VP (Visa Credit Payments)
SC (Sales Credit)	VR (Visa Credit Receipts)

Using Search

It is sometimes handy to reduce the number of records displayed in the Nominal Ledger window or on your reports to only those that match a specific criteria. This will save you having to look through many records for the information needed. For example, to list only control accounts in the Nominal Ledger window:

 Click Search in the Nominal Ledger window

Select Where, choose Account Type Code & Is Equal To

Select Control Account from the drop down list

Click on the Apply button, then click Close to finish

Hot tip

You can tell at a glance if Search is being applied to a list because it will not display the words 'All Records' on the right side of the title bar.

Don't forget

The Number (No.) column shows the transaction number in the Audit Trail. You will need this number if you wish to amend or delete a transaction using the File, Maintenance, Corrections option.

Don't forget

Search remains applied to a list until you click the Search icon on the right hand side of the title bar.

The Journal

The Journal allows you to make transfers between any of your nominal account codes regardless of type (Asset, Liability, Income or Expenditure), provided you adhere to double-entry bookkeeping principles. It lets you enter transactions which may not be covered within the standard Sage 50 facilities.

It is a useful source of reference for these non-regular transactions and can reduce errors by providing a list (audit trail) for checking purposes. Examples of these transactions include correction of errors and transfer of monies, as well as the purchase and sale of fixed assets on credit.

As stated, the Journal follows double-entry bookkeeping principles i.e., the value of the credit transaction must equal the value of the debit transaction. Each line of the Journal Entry table represents a single transaction; therefore there must be at least two transactions in the journal (a credit and a debit).

However, this does not mean that you must post a single credit item for every single debit item. You can, for example, post several debits but only one balancing credit, and vice versa. Provided the net difference between your postings is always zero (i.e. the total value of credits equals the total value of debits), you can then post the Journal.

'Skeleton' Journals

For journals that you make regularly, payments from a bank to a credit card account for example, Sage 50 lets you save the details of that journal entry so that you can use it the next time without having to enter it all again. This is called a 'skeleton'. Some skeleton journals were set up at installation, such as the VAT Liability Transfer Journal.

To save a skeleton journal, click on the Memorise button after you have set up the journal. To load a skeleton journal, click on the Recall button, select the journal you need and click on the Load button. You can even load one of the skeleton journals provided by Sage 50, modify it to suit your needs, then save it.

Reversals

In Sage 50 you can reverse an incorrectly posted journal entry using the Reversals option from the Nominal Ledger window. Use F1 Help for a full explanation of reversing a journal.

Don't forget

The rules for debits and credits are as follows: Debit the account which receives the value; Credit the account which gives the value.

Don't forget

If you post a journal entry incorrectly, Sage 50 lets you use the Reversals button from the Journals toolbar to remove the entry. You can then simply re-enter the journal correctly. Just click on the Reversals button and follow the prompts to print the Nominal Ledger Day Book and backup your data before you process the reversal.

Reversals

Making a Journal Entry

Here is an example of how you would make a journal entry for a transfer of funds between your bank account and business building society account.

1 From the Nominal Ledger toolbar, click Journals

2 Use the Calendar button if a different date is required

3 Enter details for both the credit and debit transactions. Reference is optional

4 Note, the default Tax code of T9 is entered for you

5 Check total Debit and Credit are equal and a zero balance is displayed in the Balance box

Nominal Ledger Journals

Reference	Posting Date					Balance	
TRANS	11/10/2008					0.00	
N/C	Name	Dept	Details	T/C	Debit	Credit	
1210	Bank Deposit Account	000	Transfer	T9	0.00	650.00	
1220	Building Society Account	000	Transfer	T9	650.00	0.00	
					650.00	650.00	

Save Discard Memorise Recall Print List   Close

6 To process your journal click Save, or Discard to cancel

7 Click Close to return to Nominal Ledger window

Note that Sage 50 will not automatically calculate VAT, or post it to the VAT Control Account. If VAT is required, enter each VAT element as a separate line, with a debit or credit to the appropriate VAT Control Account.

Beware

When you make a manual journal entry, VAT is neither calculated for you nor posted to the VAT control account.

Hot tip

If you use a journal entry regularly save it as a Skeleton using the Memorise button, so you can re-create it quickly and easily later.

Memorise

Beware

Before saving the Journal, always ensure the Balance box shows zero. If the value of the credit transactions does not equal the value of the debit transactions, then Sage 50 issues a warning and will not let you save the Journal.

Setting up Prepayments

To adjust statements and reports for any payments which have to be made in advance, for example rent or insurance, there is a Prepayments option available from the Nominal Ledger window. This allows for a payment to be shown as spread over the number of months it refers to, not just the month it was paid in.

After setting up a prepayment, when you run the Month End procedure the correct monthly figure is posted to the appropriate account. All you have to do is to remember to post a suitable payment for the full amount (i.e. from the bank) to the appropriate nominal account.

1. From the Nominal Ledger toolbar, click Prepay to bring up the Prepayments window

2. Enter relevant nominal account code or use Finder button

3. Enter Details, Net Value of prepayment and number of Months prepayment covers (maximum of twelve)

IHI Prepayments

N/C	Insurance				Current Item	4
PRP	Prepayments				No Of Items	4

N/C	Details	Dept	Prepayment N/C	Value	Months	Monthly Amount	sted
7100	Rent Prepayment	000	1103	1800.00	4	450.00	4
7100	Rent Prepayment	000	1103	2000.00	4	500.00	4
7100	Rent Prepayment	000	1103	2500.00	4	625.00	3
8204	Prepaid Insurance	000	1103	3250.00	12	270.83	0

| Save | Wizard | Print List | | Close |

4. Note that the monthly rate is entered for you

5. Click Save to accept prepayment details

6. Click Close to return to Nominal Ledger window

Setting up Accruals

The Accruals option allows the accounts to be adjusted for any payments you make in one accounting period which in fact relate to a previous period, such as a gas or electricity bill.

In this example, the transaction would be entered using the Accrual and Gas or Electricity accounts. When the charges actually fall due and the bill is paid, the payment transaction is applied to the Accrual account, not the Gas or Electricity account.

As with the prepayments option, the accruals are posted as part of your month end procedure using the Period End, Month End option. This procedure automatically updates the audit trail and nominal accounts records.

Hot tip

The Post column shows how many postings have been made using the Month End Post prepayment option.

1. From the Nominal Ledger window click Accrual

2. Enter nominal account code, or use the Finder button

3. Enter Details, the estimated total Net Value of accrual and number of Months for the accrual

Don't forget

No accounting takes place when accrual details are saved. Journal Entry postings are only made when the Month End, Post Accruals option is run.

53

Accruals window

N/C	Details	Dept	Accrual N/C	Value	Months	Monthly Amount	sted
7502	Telephone Accrual	000	2109	200.00	4	50.00	4
7502	Telephone Accrual	UUU	2109	225.00	4	56.25	4
7502	Telephone Accrual	000	2109	300.00	4	75.00	3
7201	Gas Accrual	000	2109	650.00	3	216.67	0

N/C: Gas   ACR: Accruals   Current Item: 4   No Of Items: 4

Save   Wizard   Print List   Close

4. Monthly accrual is calculated for you

5. Click Save to accept accrual details

6. Click Close to return to Nominal Ledger window

Hot tip

If you have already set up some Accrual entries, these appear in the Accruals window when it opens. Just add your new Accrual at the end of the list.

The Chart of Accounts

During installation, Sage 50 created a simple Chart of Accounts suitable for standard reporting, such as Profit and Loss, Balance Sheet, Budget and Prior Year Reports.

It may be that the default account names are not suitable for your business, so the Chart of Accounts can be customised to meet your business requirements. New category types can be introduced into the accounts or current categories edited to reflect, for example, the actual items sold within your business.

1   To examine the Chart of Accounts' facilities, click COA from the Nominal Ledger window

2   If you want to look at a chart, select it from the list and click Edit

---

Chart of Accounts

Description
Default Layout of Accounts
Layout 2
Layout 3

Current: Default Layout of Accounts

[Add] [Edit] [Delete] [Current] [Copy]   [Close]

---

3   To create a new Chart of Accounts, click the Add button

4   To use a particular Chart of Accounts simply highlight it from the list and click the Current button

5   When finished, click Close to return to the Nominal Ledger window

Don't forget

The chart of Accounts is subdivided into the following default report category types:

Profit & Loss
• Sales
• Purchases
• Direct Expenses
• Overheads

Balance Sheet
• Fixed Assets
• Current Assets
• Current Liabilities
• Long Term Liabilities
• Capital & Reserves

Don't forget

Always check that the name of the layout you selected appears automatically in the 'Current' text box.

Creating a Chart of Accounts Layout

Do the following to add a new Chart of Accounts layout:

1 Click COA from the Nominal Ledger window

2 Click Add in the Chart of Accounts window

3 Enter name of your new Chart of Accounts layout

4 Click Add
to continue

New Chart of Accounts	
Name	Layout 4
	Add Cancel

5 Click on a category and change its description to that
required in your financial reports

Edit Chart of Accounts				
Title		**Category Account**		
Layout 4		Sales	Low	High
		Product Sales	4000	4099
Category Type		Export Sales	4100	4199
Category Type	Description	Sales of Assets	4200	4299
Sales	Sales	Credit Charges (Late Payments)	4400	4499
Purchases	Purchases	Other Sales	4900	4999
Direct Expenses	Direct Expenses			
Overheads	Overheads			
Fixed Assets	Fixed Assets			
Current Assets	Current Assets			
Current Liabilities	Current Liabilities			
Long Term Liabilities	Long Term Liabilities			
Capital & Reserves	Capital & Reserves			
Print Check Save				Close

6 Enter (or amend) the headings for each range of nominal
accounts in the selected category and set range of nominal
accounts to be included for each selected category in Low
& High boxes

7 Click Check to see if you've
made any errors then click
Save, or Close to discard

Chart of Accounts Layout	
Output	
○ Printer	
⊙ Preview	
○ File	
○ e-Mail	
Run Cancel	

8 To print your Chart of Accounts,
click Print, then Run

Don't forget

If you elected to create
your own chart of
accounts during the
Startup Wizard, the
default chart of accounts
will not contain any
category accounts.

55

Hot tip

Use the Check button to
quickly find any nominal
account errors in your
new layout.

Nominal Reports

To print or preview reports using the nominal data already entered into the system, use the Reports option from the Nominal Ledger. Sage 50 already supplies a considerable number of pre-installed reports to suit most needs, but you can create additional custom reports using the all new Report Designer. See Chapter 12 for more details on creating reports.

To print a Nominal Ledger report, do the following:

Hot tip

You may sometimes find it easier to select nominal accounts from the Nominal Ledger window instead of entering them in the Criteria box.

1 From the Nominal Ledger toolbar, click Reports

2 Double-click on folder & select report layout required

3 Check Output is set to Preview & click Generate Report

4 Type range details or use Calendar and Finder buttons

5 Click OK to preview report

5 The Bank

This chapter shows you how to maintain your bank account records and transactions. This includes deposits, payments, transfer of money between bank accounts and adjustments to show bank charges and interest received. It also covers reconciling your statements, processing recurring entries and the production of cheques.

The Bank Toolbar

This toolbar provides features for the recording and maintenance of bank transactions and records. You can perform adjustments, record the transfer of monies, enter receipts, produce statements and reports and even print cheques.

 Record   Opens a Bank Record

 Reconcile   Opens Bank Account Reconciliation

 Payment   Record Bank Payments

 Supplier   Record Supplier Payments

 Remittance   To Print Bank Remittances

 Batch   To Record a Batch Purchase Payment

 Receipt   Record Money Received

 Customer   Record Customer Receipts

 Transfer   Make Bank Transfers

 Recurring   Opens Recurring Entries Window

 Cash Flow   Opens the Cash Flow Window

 Statement   To Print Bank Statements

 Cheques   To Print Cheques

 Reports   To Run Bank Account Reports

Bank Accounts

There are three types of Bank accounts used in Sage 50: the Bank Account, Cash Account and Credit Card Account.

The Bank account option treats both Bank and Building Societies as bank accounts. Three bank accounts have been automatically set up to include a bank current account, a bank deposit account and a building society account.

A single Cash Account called Petty Cash has been set up, but other cash accounts can be added, for example, Emergency Cash or Additional Travel Expenses etc.

The facility to record your credit card bank details is available and allows you to monitor any credit card transactions you have made and keep track of your money. Two credit card accounts have already been set up for use.

Don't forget

Remember to have your current bank balance to hand when creating new Bank records.

To view the Bank account window:

 Select Bank from the Sage 50 navigation bar

 Click on the bank account required, then click on the appropriate icon for the function you wish to carry out

A/C	Name	Balance
1200	Bank Current Account	-3.19
1210	Bank Deposit Account	3510.00
1220	Building Society Account	507.53
1230	Petty Cash	1130.48
1240	Company Credit Card	9358.97

Bank Accounts window toolbar: New, Record, Reconcile, Payment, Supplier, Remittance, Batch, Receipt, Customer, Transfer, Recurring, Cash Flow. Print List, Duplicate, Close.

3 When finished, click Close

Bank, Cash & Credit Accounts

Sage 50 provides three types of bank accounts:

Don't forget

Your bank accounts and financial reports use nominal codes 1200 to 1299.

- Bank Account (includes both bank deposit and current account, plus a building society account).

- Cash Account (named Petty Cash).

- Credit Card Account (company credit card and credit card receipts).

These accounts can be edited to match your own details. Accounts can also be added or deleted. To set up your Bank account details:

1 From the Bank Accounts window, select account type required and click on the Record icon

2 Check details and make changes if necessary

3 Click here to enter Current Balance

Don't forget

Should the minimum balance fall below the figure entered, it will be displayed in red in the Bank Accounts window.

4 Enter Opening Balance and other details then click Save

5 Click Bank Details tab and enter any further relevant details

6 Click Save to store details, then Close

Recording Bank Payments

For recording any non-invoiced or one-off payments use the Payment option from the Bank Accounts window. Sage 50 then makes it very easy for you to keep track of where your money goes – simply select the appropriate account, enter the payment and post it.

To record Bank payments:

Hot tip

Payments to your suppliers should be entered using the Supplier option as this brings up any outstanding invoices when the supplier account is entered.

1   Click Payment from the Bank Accounts window

2   Use Finder button to enter Bank account code

3   Enter Date (and transaction Reference if required)

	Bank Payments									
Bank	Bank Current Account						Tax Rate		17.50	
N/C	Miscellaneous Purchases						Total		146.88	

Bank	Date	Ref	N/C	Dept	Project Ref	Cost Code	Details	Net	T/C	Tax
1200	11/10/2008	123456	5002	002			Plants & Flo...	125.00	T1	21.88
								125.00		21.88

Save   Discard   Calc. Net   Print Cheque   Memorise   Recall   Close

Hot tip

If you only know the Gross value of the payment, simply enter it in the Net box and click on the Calc. Net button.

4   Enter a Nominal Code for the payment to be posted to, or use the Finder button

5   Enter Details describing the payment

6   Enter amount (change Tax Code from default of T1 if necessary)

7   Click Save to post details (update the nominal ledger and the Bank account)

8   Click Close to return to the Bank Accounts window

Hot tip

Use the Discard button if you want to clear any data already entered and start again. Any entries you have already saved will not be cancelled.

Supplier Invoice Payments

The Supplier option from the Bank Accounts toolbar will provide you with a detailed transaction list of any outstanding invoice items, credit notes and payments made on account to suppliers. To record payment of a supplier invoice do the following:

1 In the Bank Accounts window, select the account required (e.g. Bank Current Account) & click the Supplier button

2 Enter supplier account code in the Payee field

3 Use Calendar button if payment date is different

4 Enter cheque number if required (See the first DON'T FORGET icon in the margin)

Supplier Payment - Bank Current Account

Bank A/C Ref `1200`   Bank Current Account   Date: `19/09/2008`   Cheque No. `100123`

Payee: `SUP001`   Superior Technologies Ltd

Nine hundred eighty-four pounds and 3 pence   £   984.03

Wizard Training Limited

No.	Type	A/c	Date	Ref	Details	T/C	Amount £	Disputed?	Payment £	Discount £
895	PI	SUP001	10/09/2008	22	Diskettes - F...	T1	316.07		316.07	0.00
896	PI	SUP001	10/09/2008	22	Disk - CDR (...	T1	189.64		189.64	0.00
897	PI	SUP001	10/09/2008	22	LP100 Laser...	T1	118.00		118.00	0.00
898	PI	SUP001	10/09/2008	22	LP200 Laser...	T1	101.14		101.14	0.00
899	PI	SUP001	10/09/2008	22	JP010 Jet Pr...	T1	259.18		259.18	0.00
900	PI	SUP001	10/09/2008	22	JP020 Jet Pr...	T1	214.93		0.00	0.00
901	PI	SUP001	10/09/2008	22	JP030 Jet Pr...	T1	204.40		0.00	0.00
902	PI	SUP001	10/09/2008	22	8mb PCI Vid...	T1	463.57		0.00	0.00
903	PI	SUP001	10/09/2008	22	16mb PCI Vi...	T1	716.42		0.00	0.00

Bank Balance   -987.22   Analysis Total   984.03

Save   Discard   Pay in Full   Wizard   Automatic   Dept.   Close

5 Enter value in Payment box for part-payment or click on Pay in Full button to enter full amount

6 Repeat Step 5 for any remaining transactions

7 Click Save to save payment details, then Close to return to the Bank Accounts wondow

Batch Purchase Payments

You can list all outstanding purchase invoices, purchase credit notes and purchase payments on account for all suppliers using the Batch option from the Bank Accounts window. The transactions are sorted in order, firstly by supplier and then by transaction number.

Outstanding transactions can be paid in three ways:

- All transactions paid in full
- Individual transactions paid in full
- Individual transactions paid in part

To record full or part payments:

1 From Bank Accounts select the account and click Batch

2 To pay ALL outstanding transactions click Pay All

	No.	Type	A/c	Date	Ref	Details	T/C	Amount	Disputed?	Payment	Discount	
	895	PI	SUP001	10/09/2008	22	Diskettes - F...	T1	316.07		0.00	0.00	
	896	PI	SUP001	10/09/2008	22	Disk - LDR (...	T1	183.04		0.00	0.00	
	897	PI	SUP001	10/09/2008	22	LP100 Laser ...	T1	118.00	0.00		0.00	
	898	PI	SUP001	10/09/2008	22	LP200 Laser ...	T1	101.14		0.00	0.00	
	899	PI	SUP001	10/09/2008	22	JP010 Jet Pri...	T1	259.18		0.00	0.00	
	900	PI	SUP001	10/09/2008	22	JP020 Jet Pri...	T1	214.93		0.00	0.00	
	901	PI	SUP001	10/09/2008	22	JP030 Jet Pri...	T1	204.40		0.00	0.00	
	902	PI	SUP001	10/09/2008	22	8mb PCI Vide...	T1	463.57		0.00	0.00	
	903	PI	SUP001	10/09/2008	22	16mb PCI Vid...	T1	716.42		0.00	0.00	

Bank Current Account — Date 19/09/2008 — Superior Technologies Ltd — Bank Balance -3.19 — Total 0.00

Save | Discard | Pay in Full | Pay All | Dept. | Print List | Close

3 To make INDIVIDUAL full payments, select a transaction and click on the Pay in Full button

4 For a PART PAYMENT simply enter the amount in the Payment box

5 When finished click Save, or Discard to start again

6 Click Close

Hot tip

You can pay a transaction either in full or part.

Don't forget

All outstanding transactions can be paid in full in one go using the Pay All button, but note that there will only be one posting.

Don't forget

If any of the selected transactions are in dispute Sage 50 displays a warning message.

Bank Receipts

To record any non-invoiced or miscellaneous payments you receive, the Receipts option from the Bank Accounts window is used. These items are allocated a specific nominal code for analysis purposes so a check can be made on monies received.

To enter receipt of money:

1 From the Bank Account window click the Receipt icon

2 In Bank Receipts select the appropriate Bank account

3 Ensure the required Date is entered

Bank Receipts

Bank	Bank Current Account
N/C	Prepayments
Tax Rate	17.50
Total	89.54

Bank	Date	Ref	N/C	Dept	Project Ref	Details	Net	T/C	Tax
1200	11/10/2008	100876	1103	001		Adjustment	76.20	T1	13.34

	Net	Tax
	76.20	13.34

Save Discard Calc. Net Memorise Recall Close

4 Enter a suitable Reference, such as a cheque number

5 Select a Nominal Account Code to post the receipt to and give Details

6 Enter the Net value

7 Repeat Steps 2–6 to record further receipts, then click Save to post transactions

8 When finished, Close all windows

Recording Customer Receipts

The Customer option from the Bank Accounts window is used to record money received from your customers. When the customer's account reference is entered, any outstanding invoices appear automatically in the Customer Receipt window.

To record full or part payments:

 1 From the Bank Accounts window, select the bank account required and click Customer

2 Enter a customer Account Code to display all items not fully paid for that customer

3 Check Date and enter a paying in Reference, if possible

65

Customer Receipt - Bank Current Account

Bank Details		Customer Details		Receipt Details	
Account Ref	1200	Account	BUS001	Date	09/06/2008
Name	Bank Current Account	Name	Business Exhibitions	Amount	1779.98
Balance	-6749.22			Reference	100082

No.	Type	A/c	Date	Ref	Details	T/C	Amount £	Disputed?	Receipt £	Discount £
607	SA	BUS001	25/03/2008	44555	Payment on A	T9	100.00		100.00	0.00
1299	SI	BUS001	30/03/2008	49	PC Combo Pa...	T1	1546.59		1546.59	0.00
1300	SI	BUS001	30/03/2008	49	SIMM 32mb 1...	T1	154.67		154.67	0.00
1301	SI	BUS001	30/03/2008	49	Copy Paper ...	T1	178.72		178.72	0.00
1302	SI	BUS001	30/03/2008	49	JP010 Jet Prin...	T1	144.35		0.00	0.00
1303	SI	BUS001	30/03/2008	49	Rubber Bands...	T1	12.37		0.00	0.00
1304	SI	BUS001	30/03/2008	49	JP030 Jet Prin...	T1	129.92		0.00	0.00
1307	SI	BUS001	05/04/2008	74	Whiteboard - ...	T1	4536.68		0.00	0.00

| | Analysis Total | 1779.98 |

[Save] [Discard] [Pay in Full] [Wizard] [Automatic] [Dept.]   [Close]

---

4 If FULL payment has been received select a transaction and click Pay in Full

5 If this is a PART payment enter the amount received

6 Enter any further receipts then click Save to process them

7 When finished, Close all windows

Bank Transfers

Sometimes you will need to transfer money from one bank account to another. You can record this using the Transfer option from the Bank Accounts window or by making a journal entry.

To make a bank transfer do the following:

1 From the Bank Accounts window, select the bank you wish to move the money from

2 Click Transfer to open the Bank Transfer window

Don't forget

You can also record a Bank Transfer through a journal entry.

3 Enter Nominal Code of the Bank you are transferring to

4 Enter a Reference and appropriate Details

5 Check the date in the Date box & enter transfer amount

Don't forget

Sage 50 enters today's date in the Date box for you, but this can be altered if necessary.

6 Click Save to process or Discard to start again

7 Click Close to finish, then Close again

Recurring Entries

For payments which remain consistent and are paid on a monthly basis, for example rent and electricity, the Recurring option can be used from the Bank Accounts window. This feature is also useful for standing orders and direct debits and prevents payments such as these from being overlooked. Each month, these transactions need posting to update your banks and ledgers.

If there are any outstanding recurring entries, Sage 50 reminds you on startup and asks if you wish to post them. To add a recurring entry:

1   Select Recurring from the Bank Accounts window and Click Add

2   Enter transaction type from the list box

3   Enter the Bank Account Code

4   Enter a Nominal Code to post the transaction to

5   Give Reference & Details, then enter Posting Frequency data

6   Enter Net amount and check the Tax Code

7   Click OK to return to the Recurring Entries window

8   Click Process and Process All to process the recurring entries, then click Close to finish

Beware

Note that recurring entries need processing each month before you can run the Month or Year End procedures.

Don't forget

Sage 50 will only let you post journal credits when you post journal debits of the same value, and vice versa.

Don't forget

The Last Posted box always remains blank until the new entry is saved and processed.

Hot tip

If you need to stop a monthly payment simply click the Suspend Posting box. This is handy for those payments which do not need posting every month.

67

Generating Cheques

This feature provides you with the ability to print cheques automatically for a particular bank account. All Purchase Payments (type PP) and Purchase Payments on Account (type PA) transactions not previously printed and with blank references are listed in the Print Cheques window. This is how to print cheques using the cheque generator:

Beware

If no transactions are selected, the program will print cheques for ALL the transactions.

1 From the Bank Accounts window, select the required bank account and click on the Cheques button

2 Allocate a new Cheque Number if required

3 Select transactions requiring cheques

Hot tip

You can now print a cheque for a supplier without first having to set up an account.

4 Click Print Cheques

5 Select layout required, then click Run

6 Click Yes if cheques printed correctly, then Close

The Bank Statement

Sage 50 provides you with the facility to print your bank statements out at any time, showing all reconciled bank payments and receipts. These statements show the transactions made to and from each bank account, and prove useful for cross-referencing purposes when checking for any transaction omissions or additions. To print a report in bank statement format:

 1 From the Bank Accounts window select the desired account and click on Statement

2 Select Preview from Output options and Click Run

3 Enter Transaction Date range here and click OK to preview

4 Click Print, then OK from the print dialog box

5 Click here when finished

Print Output

Output
- ○ Printer
- ⊙ Preview
- ○ File
- ○ e-Mail

Run   Cancel

Criteria

Criteria Values

Enter the values to use for the criteria in this report

Transaction Date   Between (inclusive) ▾ 01/09/2008 ▾ and 11/10/2008 ▾

Preview a sample report for a specified number of records

September, 2008

Mon	Tue	Wed	Thu	Fri	Sat	Sun
16	26	27	28	29	30	31
1	2	3	4	5	6	7
8	9	10	11	12	13	14
15	16	17	18	19	20	21
22	23	24	25	26	27	28
29	30	1	2	3	4	5

Today: 11/10/2008

Help   Cancel

Bank Statement - Prev

Open | Export | Print | Page Setup | Printer Offsets | Email | Zoom In | Zoom Out | Close | Goto Page 1

Date: 11/10/2008
Time: 12:57:27   **Bank Statement**   Page: 1

1200
Bank Current Account   Wizard Training Limited
Currency: Pound Sterling   Wizard House
                                                  10 High Street
Book Balance: £   3375.18   Anytown
                                                  Anyshire
                                                  AA1 2ZZ

Date From: 01/09/2008
Date To: 11/10/2008

No	Date	Ref	Details	Payments £	Receipts £	Balance £
			B/Fwd Balance			-8,529.20
1347	02/09/2008	001134	Sales Receipt		2,533.31	-5,995.89
1348	09/09/2008	100332	Purchase Payment	76.98		-6,072.87
1350	15/09/2008	101552	Sales Receipt		10,194.30	4,121.43

Page 1 of 1   100%

Bank Account Reconciliation

Bank reconciliation is the process of matching up your computer bank records and transactions with those shown on the statements received from your bank.

The Bank Reconciliation window displays transactions which have not been previously reconciled. After entering the date of the statement, you can work through your bank statement matching the transactions recorded in Sage 50. If necessary, you should make any adjustments needed to ensure that Sage 50 bank accounts accurately reflect the transactions processed by your actual bank. To reconcile a bank account:

Don't forget

Before you select any transactions to reconcile, always check that the opening balance shown in the Bank Reconciliation window is the same as the opening balance on your actual bank statement.

70

1 From the Bank Accounts window select the bank account to be reconciled, then click Reconcile

2 Enter the closing balance of your bank statement

3 Enter date of the bank statement, complete details, then Click OK

Statement Summary

Bank	1200 — Bank Current Account
Statement Reference :	152
Ending Balance :	-8529.20 Statement Date : 11/10/2008

Interest Earned :
Amount : 0.00 Date : 01/10/2008 NC :

Account Charges :
Amount : 0.00 Date : 01/10/2008 NC :

OK   Cancel

4 Click each transaction that matches the bank statement

5 Click Match Transaction to add transactions to lower pane

Beware

A bank account cannot be reconciled if the check box No Bank Reconciliation is ticked on the bank record.

6 Check that the Reconcile and Statement End balances match, then click Save

7 Click Close

Bank reconciliation will only work correctly provided that a number of important rules are followed:

- The opening balance shown on the Bank Reconciliation window must match the opening balance on your actual bank statement

If for some reason they are different, you will need to check why and make the necessary adjustments. One way of doing this is to view the selected bank's activity from within the nominal ledger. To see if a transaction is reconciled, check the Bank column in the Audit Trail, where: R = reconciled and N = not reconciled.

- Work through your actual bank statement progressively one line at a time, clicking on the corresponding transaction entry in the Bank reconciliation window to highlight it

- If you come across a transaction on your bank statement not shown in Sage 50, you should record this transaction immediately using the Adjustments facility

- Check everything carefully. When you are satisfied that all transactions for reconciliation have been selected and any adjustments made, the Difference box should show zero

Making Adjustments

1 From the Reconciliation window, click the Add Adjustment button

2 Enter the Nominal Code of the account to receive the adjustment

3 Enter adjustment details and value

4 If correct click Save, then Close

Don't forget

Thoroughly check all transactions on the bank statement against the Bank Reconciliation list. Also check that the Reconcile Balance box matches the closing statement balance.

Hot tip

As you select each transaction note that the Reconcile Balance value automatically changes.

71

Hot tip

Use the Adjustments button or Bank Payments, Receipts and Transfers to record any additional transactions shown on your bank statement, e.g. bank charges, cashpoint withdrawals etc.

Bank Reports

There is a wide range of ready-to-use bank reports provided by Sage 50. These reports outline your bank details and transactions and help you keep track of your bank finances. It is advisable that you regularly print out the standard reports, such as Day Books, once you have entered the relevant transactions.

1 From the Bank Accounts window, click Reports to bring up the Bank Reports window

2 Double-click on a folder and select the report required

3 Ensure Preview is selected

4 Click Generate Report, enter Criteria, click OK then Print

Cash Flow Window

A useful feature in Sage 50 is the cash flow display, showing outstanding payments, receipts and recurring entries.

1 From the toolbar click the Cash Flow button

2 Click Print if required

6 Products

Learn how to create and maintain records for the products you buy and sell and how to set up product codes. You will also see how to monitor stock levels, the movement of stock and how to analyse product transactions.

The Products Toolbar

The Products toolbar provides features for the recording and maintenance of product records and transactions. You have the facility to record the movement of your products and make any adjustments and/or transfer of stock. Product activity can be analysed and reports generated.

Hot tip

To quickly create a new Product record, use the New Wizard from the Product Toolbar and work through the simple step by step screens.

New

Record   Opens a Product Record

Prices   To Set up a Price List

Activity   View a Product Activity

Shortfall   To Run the Product Shortfall Generator

In   Make Stock In Adjustments

Out   Make Stock Out Adjustments

Transfer   Record Stock Transfers

Stk Take   Automatically Make Stock Adjustments

Chk BOM   Check Make-Up Capability For Stock

Returns   For Recording Stock Returns

Allocate   For Recording Stock Allocations

Labels   To Produce Product Labels

Reports   To Run Product Report

The Product Record

Sage 50 allows you to create, edit or delete records for all the products your business sells. Once these records have been set up all you need to do is enter a product code and the details will be automatically included for you on any product invoice, credit note or order you create.

From the Product Record window you can view the sales price and quantity in stock for each product. Use the Products option to:

- Create and maintain records for all products bought or sold

- Record product movements

- Analyse product transactions using tables or graphs

- Set up a Bill of Materials

- Keep track of your stock levels

From the Product Record window you can view the Sales Price and Quantity in stock for each product, together with the Product Code and Description.

1 Select Products from the Sage 50 navigation bar

2 To view Product details, select a product and click on Record

3 To finish click Close

75

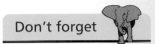

Don't forget

Opening Balances need setting up for your products. Follow the same procedures as for your customers, suppliers, nominal and bank accounts.

Beware

Once a product record has been set up, take care before deleting it, even if there is zero stock and no more is expected. It may still belong to a part allocated order.

Don't forget

Use the Stock Take option to make adjustments to your stock levels after you have completed a stock take. All you need to do is enter the current stock levels for your products and Sage 50 makes all of the necessary adjustments for you.

Product Code	Description	Sales Price	Quantity In Stock
PRN004	JP020 Jet Printer	180.00	0.00
PRN005	JP030 Jet Printer	190.00	0.00
REMEMBER01	Remember-Me Sticky Notes	3.00	11.00
REMEMBER02	Remember-Me Sticky Notes (Recycled)	3.50	8.00
REMEMBER03	Remember-Me Memo Pads	7.99	16.00
RUB001	Rubber Bands - Selection Pack (200)	6.00	21.00
SCI001	Scissors - Economy	3.00	16.00
SCN001	SCAN1000 Scanner	86.00	0.00
SCN002	SCAN2000 Scanner	189.00	0.00
TAPE001	Adhesive Tape - Brown (48mm x 60m)	2.50	28.00
TAPE002	Adhesive Tape - Brown (50mm x 66m)	2.80	12.00
TAPE003	Adhesive Tape - Clear (19mm x 33m)	0.65	10.00
TR001	LP100 Laser Printer Toner	10.00	-3.00
TR002	LP200 Laser Printer Toner	6.00	5.00
TR003	JP010 Jet Printer Cartridge	18.00	14.00
TR004	JP020 Jet Printer Cartridge	15.00	19.00
TR005	JP030 Jet Printer Cartridge	14.00	8.00
TRAY001	Letter Trays - 3 pack (Black)	7.00	7.00
TRAY002	Letter Trays - 3 pack (Pink/Brown)	7.00	7.00
TRAY003	Letter Trays - 3 pack (Grey)	7.00	14.00

2 of 105 products selected, total 4.50

Search | Swap | Clear | Delete | Copy Discount | Print List | Duplicate | Batch Change | Close

...cont'd

Entering a product record

You can update the sales price for all product items using the Global Changes option from the Tools menu.

Beware

If the Ignore Stock Levels check box is selected (ticked) on the product record, its details will not appear on some reports, i.e. Stock History.

76

Don't forget

You can save your stock take details to a file for opening at a later date, to continue with the stock take, or to view the adjustments that you previously made. Remember, however, to enter all of your stock take details before you process any transactions that would alter your stock levels. This is because your stock details may change between the date that the last stock date was saved and the next time it is re-opened.

1 From the Products window click on Record

2 Type a unique Product Code and press Tab

3 Enter Description, check the Nominal sales & VAT code

4 Enter Sales Price here

5 Click on O/B button then Yes to save changes

6 Check for correct Date & enter Quantity

7 Enter Cost Price of the Product

8 Click Save, then Close to return to the Products window

Entering details onto the Product Record

Whilst the Product Record has been designed to accept a considerable amount of detail, not every item is applicable to all products. However, to make reporting more accurate later, you should try and include as much detail as possible about a product when adding records.

Not all of the boxes on the Product Record will accept user entry though. Sage 50 calculates or generates the following information and enters it for you. It cannot be directly edited.

Allocated — This figure shows the quantity of the product which has been partly or fully allocated on the sales order, but which has not yet been despatched.

Free Stock — Sage 50 calculates the Free Stock as being the In Stock total minus the Allocated stock total.

On Order — Using the Purchase Orders option, this is the quantity of the product which has been put 'on order'.

Last Ord Qty — This shows the amount of stock ordered when the last purchase order for this product was put 'on order'.

Last Ord Date — This shows the date of the last purchase order raised for this product after being put on order.

Cost Price — This is the latest cost price for the product item, entered using the Opening Balance option, the Adjustments In option, Purchase Order Processing or the Global Changes option (useful for updating cost prices for all or selected product items).

When running financial or management reports, you must remember that Sage 50 will use this latest price even though products already in stock may have actually cost more or less. This may, on occasion, give distorted figures, such as when calculating the total cost value of a product item in stock.

Hot tip

If stock level falls below the re-order level, the item appears red in the Products window and also appears on the Re-order report.

77

Beware

If you do not enter a Cost Price in the Opening Product Setup box, the product cost is recorded as zero. This could affect some of your finance reports later.

Product Defaults

To save entering repetative details and to make the process of creating new product records easier, Sage 50 includes the facility to set up various product defaults.

Whenever a new product record is created, certain regular details, e.g. Nominal Code, Tax Code, Department etc, are asked for. If you use a recording system where these codes remain the same for most of your products, default settings can be set up which will then appear automatically in each new product record without you having to enter them every time. To set up product defaults:

Don't forget

If you set the Unit DP to a value greater than 2, the net amount on any product invoice created will still be rounded to 2 decimal places.

1   From the Sage 50 menu bar, first select Settings, then Product Defaults

2   Enter the Nominal Code to be used by default whenever you create orders and product invoices

3   Select the VAT rate & Purchase code, if relevant

4   Enter Unit of Sale, e.g. 'each' or 'box', then choose Category and Department as required

5   Enter number of decimal places for Quantity and Unit sale price

Hot tip

Use the Descriptions tab to quickly set up your own product discount names.

6   Click OK to save or Cancel to discard any changes

Product Defaults

Details | Descriptions

Defaults

Sales Nominal Code	4000
Tax Code	T1 17.50
Purchase Nominal Code	5000
Unit of Sale	Each
Category	1 Paper Products
Department	007
Image Options	Maintain Image Size

Decimal Precision

Quantity D.P.	2
Unit D.P.	2

OK   Cancel

Using Search

Using Search speeds up the process of searching for specific product records, for example to show products which match a particular description, or those below the re-order stock level. The following example shows how to set up a search to restrict Product Records to only those with less than 50 in stock:

 Click the Search button in the bottom left hand corner of the Products window to bring up the Search window

 Click Where in the first column

3 Select Quantity in stock in this field

4 Select Is Less Than in the Condition column

5 Enter 50 in the Value field

6 Click Apply & Close to return to the Products window

7 Note that only records matching the search are displayed. The title bar indicates the Search is applied

8 To cancel the search and show all records, click this icon

Hot tip

The calculator button is a quick and handy way of making an entry in the Value field.

Hot tip

Use the Save button to record searches you use frequently. You can then recall these as required from the Search window.

Don't forget

Search remains applied to a list until you click the search icon on the right hand side of the title bar:

Bill of Materials

This term relates to a product you hold in stock made up from other products you keep. The made up product is sometimes known as a product assembly and is said to have a Bill of Materials. For example, a first aid kit is a product assembly consisting of various components – bandages, tablets, plasters, etc.

For businesses selling a product made up of other products, it is useful to set up a Bill of Materials. In Sage 50 this feature keeps track of stock levels and can automatically calculate how many products you can make up for sale from the stock you currently hold and at what cost price. To set up a Bill of Materials for a product do the following:

1 From the Products window, select the product you wish to set up a Bill of Materials for, then click Record

2 Click the BOM tab from the Product Record

3 Enter Product Code for each item

4 Enter quantity required for product assembly

5 Click Refresh to see how many you can make from stock

6 Click Save to store, or Discard to start again

7 Click Close

80

Viewing Transactions

The Sales Tab

You can use this dialog box to view the sales value and quantity sold for your selected product during the financial year on a month by month basis. With a record selected:

 1 From the Product Record click on the Sales tab

2 Click Close when finished

Hot tip

To amend values for all, or a selected group of products within the Product Record, use the Global Changes option from the Tools menu.

Product Record - 200gb Hard Drive

Details | Memo | BOM | Sales | Graph | Activity | Discount | Web

Month	Sales Cost	Actuals	Budgets	Prior Year	Actuals	Budgets	Prior Year
		Sales Value			Quantity Sold		
Late Adj.	811.30	959.74	0.00	0.00	14.00	0.00	0.00
Apr	1464.00	1800.00	0.00	0.00	24.00	0.00	0.00
May	1037.00	1275.00	0.00	0.00	17.00	0.00	0.00
Jun	1830.00	2250.00	0.00	0.00	30.00	0.00	0.00
Jul	915.00	1125.00	0.00	0.00	15.00	0.00	0.00
Aug	1037.00	1275.00	0.00	0.00	17.00	0.00	0.00
Sep	1281.00	1575.00	0.00	0.00	21.00	0.00	0.00
Oct	0.00	0.00	0.00	0.00	0.00	0.00	0.00
Nov	0.00	0.00	0.00	0.00	0.00	0.00	0.00
Dec	0.00	0.00	0.00	0.00	0.00	0.00	0.00
Jan	0.00	0.00	0.00	0.00	0.00	0.00	0.00
Feb	0.00	0.00	0.00	0.00	0.00	0.00	0.00
Mar	0.00	0.00	0.00	0.00	0.00	0.00	0.00
Future	0.00	0.00	0.00	0.00	0.00	0.00	0.00
Totals	8375.30	10259.74	0.00	0.00	138.00	0.00	0.00

Date Of Last Sale 11/10/2008

Save | Discard | Delete | Previous | Next | Print List | Close

Hot tip

Use a range of 2D and 3D chart types to compare how you did last year compared to this year's budgets.

Product Discounts

1 From the Product Record click on the Discount tab

2 Enter quantities for customer to qualify for a discount & % Discount

3 Discounted value is calculated for you

Product Record - 200gb Hard Drive

Details | Memo | BOM | Sales | Graph | Activity | Discount | Web

Discount A | Discount B | Discount C | Discount D | Discount E

Discount	Quantity	Discount %	Discounted Value
Level 1		10.00	67.50
Level 2	10.00	15.00	63.75
Level 3	30.00	20.00	60.00
Level 4	100.00	25.00	56.25
Level 5	0.00	0.00	0.00
Level 6	0.00	0.00	0.00
Level 7	0.00	0.00	0.00
Level 8	0.00	0.00	0.00
Level 9	0.00	0.00	0.00
Level 10	0.00	0.00	0.00

Copy Matrix

Save | Discard | Delete | Previous | Next | Print List | Close

4 Click Save, then Close

Hot tip

Use the Copy Matrix button to copy the discount structure from another already discounted product.

Product Activity

Details regarding adjustments of goods in and out, stock transfers, current quantities in stock, on order and allocated prove invaluable when trying to fulfil orders or analyse and track stock movement.

You can decide when you no longer wish to retain certain transactions on your system by using the Clear Stock option. This facility enables transactions to be cleared from your Product History prior to a specific date.

It is important that you understand the following terms when trying to calculate the availability of stock and to understand the product reports produced by Sage 50:

Tp: A code to identify the type of transaction, where:

AI	=	Adjustment In
AO	=	Adjustment Out
MI	=	Movement In (product transfer only)
MO	=	Movement Out (product transfer only)
GR	=	Goods Returned (via credit notes)
GO	=	Goods Out (via sales orders and product invoices)
GI	=	Goods In (via purchase orders)
DI	=	Damages In
DO	=	Damages Out
WO	=	Write Off

Used: This is the sum of all the AO (Adjustments Out), GO (Goods Out) and MO (Movements Out) quantities for the product within the specified date range.

Cost: If the transaction line refers to an AI (Adjustment In), GI (Goods In), GR (Goods Returned) or MI (Movement In), this shows the cost price.

Sale: Where a transaction line refers to an AO (Adjustment Out), GO (Goods Out) or GR (Goods Returned), this shows the sales price.

Don't forget

Where activities have been cleared at the month end, they will be shown as carried forward totals with a Ref. of O/BAL, usually at the top of the list.

Hot tip

To clear stock transactions, choose the Period End option from the Tools menu and click the Clear Stock option. Adjustments made are brought forward as opening balances, showing quantities used, in AI and MI.

Don't forget

Use the type code WO for recording faulty goods as write-offs.

...cont'd

Qty on Order: This is the product quantity which has been placed on order using the Purchase Order option, but not yet delivered.

Qty Allocated: This shows the product quantity that has been allocated to sales orders using the Sales Order Processing option.

Qty in Stock: This is the sum of all the AI (Adjustments In), MI (Movements In), GI (Goods In) and GR (Goods Received), less the quantity used for the specified period.

Qty Available: The Quantity in Stock less Quantity Allocated.

To view Activity from the Products window:

1 Click on the product or products required

2 From the Products toolbar click the Activity button

3 Click here to select a diferent Date Range

	Activity								
Product	HAR002		Description	200gb Hard Drive					
Cat Number	10		Category	Computer Hardware					

Show: Custom Range... Date: 01/01/1980 to 31/12/2099 Type: All

Ty	Da		ils	Project Ref	Cost Code	Qty In	Qty Out	Qty Used	Cost Price	Sales Price
AI	31	February	b Hard Drive			3.00		3.00	61.00	
GO 11	March	ds Out				4.00			61.00	71.25
GI	28/08/2008 11	Goods In			14.00		14.00	54.90		
MO 28/08/2008		PC003					5.00		54.90	
MO 28/08/2008		PC004					5.00		54.90	
GO 11/09/2008 23	Goods Out					3.00		54.90	71.25	
GO 11/09/2008 40	Goods Out					3.00		61.00	60.56	
GI 30/09/2008 31	Goods In				20.00		11.00	54.90		
MO 30/09/2008		PC003					4.00		54.90	
GO 14/10/2008 56	Goods Out					4.00		54.90	69.83	

Quantity on Order 0.00 Quantity in Stock 9.00

Quantity Allocated 0.00 Quantity Available 9.00

Previous Next Print List Close

4 Click Previous or Next if more than one product selected

5 Click Close when finished

Hot tip

Viewing a product's activity is also available using the Activity tab from within the Product Record window.

Hot tip

Use the Transaction Type range facility in the Date Range window to refine and speed up your search of Product activity.

Hot tip

Use the Finder button to select another Product Code if required.

Product Adjustments

The In and Out options from the Product window are used to record adjustments to your product's stock levels, such as when stock is received into stores, an order is returned, or stock is taken out as damaged.

The In button is used to enter any increase in a product's available stock, whilst the Out option is for recording a decrease.

To make Adjustments In

 From the Products window click the In option

Enter Product Code, Date & Ref, Quantity in and enter the new Cost if changed

Click Save to store changes and Close

The Out button is used to record any miscellaneous product movements which decrease a product's available stock level and where no product invoice has been raised.

To make Adjustments Out

Click on Out

Enter the Product Code and Quantity, then click Save

Hot tip

If there is a discrepancy after a stock take, just enter the stock adjustment using the Stock Take option.

Don't forget

Cost prices are important to the valuation of the stock as product levels are controlled on a first in, first out basis. Always enter cost prices, therefore, to achieve accurate valuation.

Beware

You cannot use the Returns option for non-stock or service items.

Product Transfers

This feature is used for increasing the In Stock quantity of Product Assemblies using components currently in stock. The Product Assemblies are set up using the Bill of Materials option (see page 80).

When using the Stock Transfers option the cost price for each Product Assembly is calculated for you by Sage 50, by adding together the cost price of each component.

To make a product transfer from the Products window:

1 Click on the Transfer button

2 Click on the Product Code Finder button

Stock Transfers window showing Product Code PC005, PC Combo Pack 5, Date 11/10/2008, with the Products finder listing: PC003 PC Combo Pack 3, PC004 PC Combo Pack 4, PC005 PC Combo Pack 5, PC006 PC Combo Pack 6, PEN001 Ball Point Pen - Black, PEN002 Ball Point Pen - Blue, PEN003 Ball Point Pen - Red.

3 Select the desired Product Assembly Code & click OK

4 Check Details and Date

5 Enter Quantity required, Sage 50 warns you if insufficient stock available to make the product assembly

6 Click Save to record entries or Discard to start again

7 Click Close

Beware

You can only use a product code which has been previously set up to be a product assembly using the BOM option.

Don't forget

If you do not have sufficient stock of components to make up the quantity you have entered, Sage 50 will display a warning.

Hot tip

Quickly check your component stock levels by clicking on the Shortfall button on the Products toolbar to bring up the Shortfall Generator window (Accounts Plus and Professional only).

Shortfall

Hot tip

Use Check BOM to quickly check which stock items and components are needed to complete orders.

Product Reports

The Stock Reports option allows you to print out a wide range of useful pre-prepared product related reports. These reports show such things as product details and movements, and will help you to keep track of what you have in stock, its financial value etc.

Additional product reports tailored to your business needs can be created using the Report Designer (See Chapter 12). To run a Product Report:

Hot tip

Use the Product Audit Trail to quickly track the movement of stock.

1 From the Products window click Reports

2 Double-click on the required folder and select a report

Don't forget

If you selected to print the report, the Windows Print dialog box appears. Use this to select which pages to print and to change your printer settings if necessary.

3 Ensure Preview selected & click Generate Report

4 Enter any required Criteria

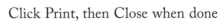

5 Click OK to generate report

6 Click Print, then Close when done

Hot tip

You can easily generate labels for your products by clicking on the Labels button from the Products window toolbar.

7 Invoices

This chapter shows you how to produce invoices and credit notes for your products and services. Customers, Products and Nominal Accounts are directly linked to Invoicing so the invoices produced automatically update the relevant ledgers.

The Invoicing Toolbar

This toolbar provides facilities for generating invoices, quotes, proformas and credit notes for the goods you sell and the services you provide. Ledgers can be automatically updated, transactions printed out and reports generated for analysis.

 New/Edit   To Create or View an Invoice, Pro-forma or Credit Note

 Recurring   To Open Saved Skeleton or Recurring Transactions

 Print   To Print an Invoice or a Credit Note

 Update   To Update Ledgers

 Labels   To Print Invoice Labels

 Reports   To Run Invoicing Reports

Invoicing

Processing manually generated invoices, or batch invoicing, i.e. items not generated using Sage 50, has already been referred to in Chapters 2 and 3. Briefly, Chapter 2 (Customers) explains how to log invoices and credit notes within the system after they have been produced and sent to customers. Chapter 3 (Suppliers) explains how to record the invoices and credit notes you receive from your suppliers.

Invoicing deals with Sage 50 generated invoices, of which there are two basic types. First there is the Product Invoice, which is used for invoicing customers for the products you sell. Each line of the invoice can be used for recording specific product items. Early discount settlement can be offered on these invoices and carriage charges applied.

Meanwhile, the Service Invoice is used to invoice customers you have provided a service for. An unlimited amount of text can be entered into the invoice describing the services supplied. Discount settlement can be applied and carriage charges recorded.

As Sage 50 generates these invoices, all the relevant details are automatically recorded and posted for you when you are ready. For invoices where the same information is entered regularly, the Memorise option saves the invoice as a template. This template can then be recalled when required and updated with the new information, saving valuable time.

Within Invoicing is the facility to generate credit notes for your customers, where products or services for example, have not been received or had to be returned. When these transactions are posted, the ledgers will be updated automatically.

You do, of course, need to keep track of your invoicing. Use the report facility regularly to print out a list of Invoices not yet printed or posted, or to check on stock requirements or shortfalls for the invoices you have generated using this Invoicing option.

In older versions of Sage 50, the Invoicing toolbar contained separate buttons for Product and Service Invoices and Credit Notes. With version 2008 the toolbar contains only one New/Edit button. The type of Invoice or Credit Note is then selected from the Type and Format boxes in the Invoice window.

Don't forget

Sage 50 generates invoice numbers in sequence, normally starting at 1. However, you can start with your own numbering system, of up to seven digits. This will be incremented for you each time a new invoice is generated.

Don't forget

Your Invoices remain in the Invoicing window list box until removed using the Delete option.

The Product Invoice

To invoice your customers for the products you sell, use the New/Edit option from the Invoicing toolbar, then select the Product option in the drop down list in the Type box. To create an Invoice click Modules, then Invoicing, from the menu bar and do the following:

1 Click New/Edit on the Invoicing toolbar. Invoice and Product appears in Type & Format by default

2 Enter the tax point date if different

3 Type Sales Order No. if applicable

4 Enter Customer Account Code, Customer details appear

5 Enter the Product Code (use the Finder button), followed by the Quantity

Product Invoice

Product Code	Description	Quantity	Price £	Net £	V.A.T. £
BOARD001	Whiteboard - Drywipe (900 x 1200)	3.00	16.50	48.26	8.45
ENV003	Envelope - Brown (110 x 220) Plain	5.00	6.75	32.91	5.76
PAPER004	Inkjet Paper - Premium Grade	10.00	4.50	43.88	7.68

Business Exhibitions
44 Keswick Way
Penrith
Cumbria
CA97 9RT

Type: Invoice — Product Invoice
Format: Product — Inv.No. <AutoNumber>
Date: 11/10/2008 — Order No
A/C: BUS001 — Item No. Item 3 of 3

Deduction	Description	Net £
Net Value Discount		0.00

Total GBP £ 125.05 — 21.89
Carriage GBP £ 0.00 — 0.00
Gross GBP £ 146.94

Less Deposit GBP £ 0.00
Amount Due GBP £ 146.94

Save · Discard · Print · Memorise · Recall · Profit · Send e-Mail · Close

6 Repeat Step 5 for further products, clicking here if you need to edit any of the product details, then click Save

7 Click Close

...cont'd

Product Invoice Order Details

You can also record useful additional Order Details on your Invoice if necessary:

1. Click on Order Details tab
2. Enter Delivery Address and any Notes if required
3. Enter Customer Order Details, especially Order No

Product Invoice Footer Details

Further details, such as Carriage and Settlement Terms, go in the Footer Details:

4. Click on Footer Details tab & enter any Carriage details
5. Record Settlement Terms as appropriate
6. Enter any Global detail if required
7. Click Save, then Close to finish

Beware

Any changes made to the delivery details are not saved back to the Customer Record.

Hot tip

For a payment which has already been received and can be allocated against a product invoice, record it using the Payment Details tab.

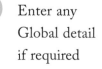
Don't forget

The Tax Analysis is now shown in the Footer Details section. In previous versions it was on the Details screen.

91

Printing an Invoice

Sage 50 gives you the option to print Invoices or Credit Notes either immediately, or at a later date. To print straight away after you have entered all of the details, instead of clicking Save (the Invoice is automatically saved for you) do the following:

Don't forget

When using the Invoicing option to create invoices and credit notes, you can choose either to print straight away or save them as a batch for printing later using the Print option on the Invoicing Toolbar.

Hot tip

Batching invoices or credit notes is useful if you only have one printer. Simply load the correct stationery in the printer, then print them all in one go.

Beware

If no records are selected from the list in the Invoicing window, all non-printed invoices or credit notes will be printed by default.

92

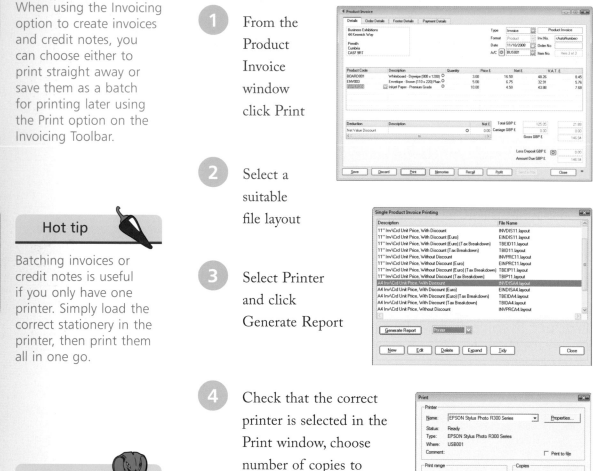

1. From the Product Invoice window click Print

2. Select a suitable file layout

3. Select Printer and click Generate Report

4. Check that the correct printer is selected in the Print window, choose number of copies to print and click OK

5. If you wish to post the invoice and Update the Ledgers select Preview then click OK, else cancel to print only

6. Click Close to finish

The Service Invoice

To invoice customers for the services you provide instead of products you sell, you should generate a Service Invoice, still using the New/Edit button from the Invoicing Toolbar. An unlimited amount of text can be entered to describe the services provided, and each service can be analysed to a different nominal account. Settlement discounts can be applied, as can carriage charges.

As with Product Invoices, a Service Invoice can be saved to print later or printed straight away. When printing, you have the option to update the ledgers at the same time or leave till later.

1 Click New/Edit on the Invoicing toolbar and select Service in the Format field

2 Change date if different & enter Sales Order No.

3 Enter Customer Account Code, Customer details appear

4 Type service Details here & enter Net cost

93

Service Invoice

Details	Order Details	Footer Details	Payment Details

Stevenson & Smith
Acorn Close
Hale
Altrincham
Cheshire
C39 3TD

Type: Invoice — Service Invoice
Format: Service
Inv No. <AutoNumber>
Date: 11/10/2008
Order No. WIZ2234
A/C: STE001
Item No. Item 2 of 2

Details	Amount £	Net £	V.A.T. £
Sage Training Course - Full Day		700.00	700.00	122.50
Refreshments		100.00	100.00	17.50

Deduction	Description	Net £		
Net Value Discount		0.00		

Total GBP £ 800.00 140.00
Carriage GBP £ 0.00 0.00
Gross GBP £ 940.00

Less Deposit GBP £ 0.00
Amount Due GBP £ 940.00

| Save | Discard | Print | Memorise | Recall | Send e-Mail | Previous | Close | » |

5 Repeat Step 4 as necessary, then click Save

6 Click Close

Service Invoice Order Details

You can record useful additional Order Details on your Service Invoice if required:

If you make a mistake, simply click Discard and start again.

1 Click on Order Details tab

2 Enter Delivery Address and any Notes if required

3 Enter Customer Order Details, especially Order No

Any changes made to the delivery details are not saved back to the Customer Record.

Service Invoice Footer Details

You can record details such as Carriage and Settlement Terms in the Footer Details box:

4 Click on Footer Details tab & enter any Carriage details

5 Record Settlement Terms as appropriate

For payments you have received which can be allocated against the invoice, record the details using the Payment Details tab.

6 Enter any Global detail if required

7 Click Save, then Close to finish

The Skeleton Invoice

For information that is regularly repeated when creating an invoice, use the Memorise option to store the invoice as a template. You can then recall this template as and when required, and update it with the new information, thus saving valuable time and reduce keying errors.

This facility is available for both Product and Service Invoices, as well as the Product and Service Credit Notes.

1 On the Details screen enter regularly used details only, such as Customer A/C Ref. & item Details. Omit Price

Hot tip

To bring up a list of all the invoices or orders that you have saved as skeletons or recurring transactions, click the Recurring button from the Invoice toolbar.

Service Invoice

Details	Order Details	Footer Details	Payment Details

Stevenson & Smith
Acorn Close
Hale
Altrincham
Cheshire
C39 3TD

Type: Invoice — Service Invoice
Format: Service — Inv.No. <AutoNumber>
Date: 11/10/2008 — Order No
A/C: STE001 — Item No. Item 2 of 2

Details		Amount £	Net £	V.A.T. £
Sage Training Course - Full Day		700.00	700.00	122.50
Refreshments		100.00	100.00	17.50

Deduction	Description		Net £		
Net Value Discount			0.00	Total GBP £	800.00 / 140.00
				Carriage GBP £	0.00 / 0.00
				Gross GBP £	940.00
				Less Deposit GBP £	0.00
				Amount Due GBP £	940.00

| Save | Discard | Print | Memorise | Recall | Send e-Mail | Previous | Close | » |

Hot tip

A quick way to alter the date in a Date box is to use the up or down cursor keys to move through the days. Pressing Page Up or Page Down moves through the months.

2 Click Memorise

Memorise

Details
Reference: STC001
Description: Sage Training Course, Full Day

Frequency
If you would like this transaction to be automatically generated in Sage 50 Accounts, fill out the frequency details below:

Every: 0 Day(s) — Total Required: 0
Start Date: 11/10/2008 — Finish Date: Perpetual
Last Processed: — Suspended? ☐

| Save | | Cancel |

3 Enter Filename and Description then click Save

4 When you need to use a layout, click Recall

5 Select your layout from the list and click Load

Hot tip

To have Sage 50 Automatically generate this transaction for you at set regular intervals, just fill in the details in the frequency section of the Memorise window.

Product Credit Note

From time to time goods sent to customers may be returned as faulty, past an expiry date, etc, or the customer may simply have been overcharged by mistake.

Instead of correcting the original invoice, a Product Credit Note can be issued to the Customer, detailing the amount owing to them. When your ledgers are updated, the necessary postings will be made to reflect this amendment. Do the following to create a Product Credit Note:

1 Click New/Edit from the Invoicing toolbar and select Credit from the Type field

2 Check Date and enter Order Number if relevant

3 Enter Customer Code, Customer details appear

Hot tip

A VAT only credit note can be raised where a customer has been invoiced and charged tax for goods which are exempt from VAT.

Beware

In Sage 50 you must always select the Invoice Format, i.e., Product or Service, prior to entering any product or service details. Once you begin to enter these details, the Format box goes to grey and can only be changed by discarding the Invoice and starting all over again.

4 Enter the Product Code and the Quantity

5 Repeat Step 4 as required, then click Save to finish

6 Click Close

Process Recurring Transactions

Information that is regularly repeated when creating a Product or Service Invoice or Credit note can be stored and later recalled for use as required or for updating. This feature is particulary useful for any recurring transactions you may have.

If the Frequency details were entered when the recurring transaction skeleton was created and memorised, Sage 50 will remind you automatically on startup if you have any outstanding transactions for processing. You can then choose to immediately post the transactions or process them at a later date as follows:

1   Click Recurring from the Invoicing toolbar to bring up the Memorised Invoices window

2   Click Process

3   Remove tick here if an entry is not to be processed, then click Process to produce your recurring transactions

4   If any tick was removed in Step 3, click No in next window

5   Click OK in the Processing Complete window, then Cancel to close

Updating your Ledgers

After creating your invoices and credit notes, the Update function is used to transfer details to the customer and nominal ledgers and, if appropriate, to amend product records.

Sage 50 gives you the option to print the update report immediately, preview it first so that you can select only certain pages for printing, or to save the report as a file. To perform an Update, do the following:

1 From the Invoicing window select invoices/credit notes for updating

2 Click Update to display Output option

98

Invoicing

New/Edit Recurring Print Update Labels Reports

No.	Type	Date	Name	Amount	Printed	Posted
65	Inv	14/08/2008	Hausser GMBH	1975.16		Yes
66	Inv	27/08/2008	Graham Electronics	4149.09		Yes
67	Inv	27/08/2008	S D Enterprises	1239.68		Yes
68	Inv	27/08/2008	Bobs Building Supplies	4309.77		Yes
69	Inv	28/08/2008	Peter Young	2106.84	Yes	Yes
70	Srv	01/09/2008	S D Enterprises	4700.00		Yes
71	Srv	01/09/2008	Edward Stuart	2341.25		Yes
72	Srv	05/09/2008	Kinghorn & French	7398.35		Yes
73	Srv	16/09/2008	Mile Road Health Centre	585.31		Yes
74	Inv	05/10/2008	Business Exhibitions	4536.68		Yes
75	Inv	05/10/2008	Fred Briant	344.16		Yes
76	Inv	05/10/2008	Patterson & Graham Garages	1056.49		Yes
77	Inv	13/10/2008	Business Exhibitions	146.94	Yes	
78	Inv	13/10/2008	Kinghorn & French	52.68		
79	Inv	14/10/2008	Steven Stephenson	2753.31		
80	Inv	15/10/2008	Mile Road Health Centre	3336.28		
81	Inv	18/10/2008	Swan Leisure Centre	56.72		
82	Inv	19/10/2008	ABS Garages Ltd	120.11		
83	Inv	19/10/2008	John Smith Studios	55.81		
84	Inv	22/10/2008	Mikes Insurance Services	71.91		
85	Inv	22/10/2008	County Golf Supplies	444.84		

3 of 85 invoices selected, total balance: 6209.70

Search Swap Clear Delete Print List Duplicate Close

3 In the Update Ledgers window click Preview

Update Ledgers

Output

OK

Cancel

○ Printer
◉ Preview
○ File

4 Click OK to generate the update

5 On the report, click Print to bring up the Print dialog box, then click OK to print

6 Close to return to the Invoicing window, then Close again

Printing for Batch Invoicing

When you created Invoices or Credit Notes, for both Product or Service, you may have decided to leave printing them until later as a batch. This can often save time when setting up file layouts and having to change the printer stationery.

For example, you may have created four Service invoices which now need printing. You would do the following:

1 From the Invoicing window, select the invoices to print

2 Click Print

Don't forget

You can reprint your invoices as many times as you wish.

No.	Type	Date	Name	Amount	Printed	Posted
65	Inv	14/08/2008	Hausser GMBH	1975.16		Yes
66	Inv	27/08/2008	Graham Electonics	4149.09		Yes
67	Inv	27/08/2008	S D Enterprises	1239.68		Yes
68	Inv	27/08/2008	Bobs Building Supplies	4309.77		Yes
69	Inv	28/08/2008	Peter Young	2106.84	Yes	Yes
70	Srv	01/09/2008	S D Enterprises	4700.01		Yes
71	Srv	01/09/2008	Edward Stuart	2341.25		Yes
72	Srv	05/09/2008	Kingham & French	7398.35		Yes
73	Srv	18/09/2008	Mile Road Health Centre	505.31		Yes
74	Inv	05/10/2008	Business Exhibitions	4536.68		Yes
75	Inv	05/10/2008	Fred Briant	344.16		Yes
76	Inv	05/10/2008	Patterson & Graham Garages	1056.49		Yes
77	Inv	13/10/2008	Business Exhibitions	148.94	Yes	
78	Inv	13/10/2008	Kingham & French	52.68		
79	Inv	14/10/2008	Steven Stephenson	2753.31		Yes
80	Inv	15/10/2008	Mile Road Health Centre	3336.28		Yes
01	Inv	18/10/2008	Swan Leisure Centre	56.72		
82	Inv	19/10/2008	ABS Garages Ltd	120.11		Yes
83	Inv	19/10/2008	John Smith Stirling	55.81		
84	Inv	22/10/2008	Mikes Insurance Services	71.91		
85	Inv	22/10/2008	County Golf Supplies	444.84		

Hot tip

Use the Search button if you wish to print a number of invoices or credit notes that match a particular condition.

3 Select the Layout required

4 Ensure Preview is selected

5 Click on Generate Report

Description	File Name
11" Inv\Crd Unit Price, With Discount	INVDIS11.layout
11" Inv\Crd Unit Price, With Discount (Euro)	EINDIS11.layout
11" Inv\Crd Unit Price, With Discount (Euro) (Tax Breakdown)	TBEID11.layout
11" Inv\Crd Unit Price, With Discount (Tax Breakdown)	TBID11.layout
11" Inv\Crd Unit Price, Without Discount	INVPRC11.layout
11" Inv\Crd Unit Price, Without Discount (Euro)	EINPRC11.layout
11" Inv\Crd Unit Price, Without Discount (Euro) (Tax Breakdown)	TBEIP11.layout
11" Inv\Crd Unit Price, Without Discount (Tax Breakdown)	TBIP11.layout
A4 Inv\Crd Unit Price, With Discount	INVDISA4.layout
A4 Inv\Crd Unit Price, With Discount (Euro)	EINDISA4.layout
A4 Inv\Crd Unit Price, With Discount (Euro) (Tax Breakdown)	TBEIDA4.layout
A4 Inv\Crd Unit Price, With Discount (Tax Breakdown)	TBIDA4.layout
A4 Inv\Crd Unit Price, Without Discount	INVPRCA4.layout
A4 Inv\Crd Unit Price, Without Discount (Euro)	EINPRCA4.layout
A4 Inv\Crd Unit Price, Without Discount (Euro) (Tax Breakdown)	TBEIPA4.layout

Don't forget

Standard layouts can always be edited or new layouts created and saved as necessary.

6 On the preview, click Print to bring up the Windows Print dialog box, then click OK to print

7 Close to return to the Invoicing window, then Close again

Producing Reports

The Reports option allows you to produce a wide range of reports about your product and service invoices, as well as your credit notes. Use these reports regularly to keep your business up to date. For example, to print an Invoices Not Posted report:

1 Click Reports from the Invoicing toolbar

2 Double-click on folder and select report required

3 Ensure Preview is selected

4 Click Generate Report to produce report

5 Check report then click Print

| Date: | 15/10/2008 | | Wizard Training Limited | | Page: | 1 |
| Time: | 13:38:15 | | Invoices Not Posted | | | |

Number	Type	Date	A/C	Name	Amount
77	Product Invoice	13/08/2008	BUS001	Business Exhibitions	146.94
78	Product Invoice	13/08/2008	KIN001	Kinghorn & French	52.68
81	Product Invoice	18/08/2008	SWA001	Swan Leisure Centre	56.72
83	Product Invoice	19/08/2008	JSS001	John Smith Studios	55.81
84	Product Invoice	22/08/2008	MIB001	Mikes Insurance Services	71.91
85	Product Invoice	22/08/2008	CGS001	County Golf Supplies	444.84
86	Product Invoice (from SOP)	13/09/2008	BUS001	Business Exhibitions	189.03
87	Product Invoice (from SOP)	13/09/2008	SDE001	S D Enterprises	1,797.75
88	Product Invoice	11/10/2008	BUS001	Business Exhibitions	146.94
89	Product Invoice	13/10/2008	BRO001	Bronson Inc	0.00
90	Service Invoice	15/10/2008	PEL01	Palmer Energy Ltd	0.00
				End of Report	2,962.62

6 Click OK to print report, then Close all windows

8

Processing Sales Orders

Learn how to create Sales Orders and then allocate and despatch stock to these orders as well as how to keep your stock levels up-to-date.

Sales Order Processing Toolbar

The SOP toolbar provides a number of features for creating a sales order and then controlling the allocation of stock to that order. Once you are ready to deliver the stock, you can despatch it and Sage 50 will automatically handle the stock record updates. From this toolbar you can also print sales orders, whilst information regarding sales order processing can be easily obtained by using the various report layouts already provided for you.

New/Edit — To Create or View a Sales Order

Allocate — To Allocate Stock to a Sales Order

Despatch — To Despatch a Sales Order

GDN — To Record Delivery of Goods to your Customers

Amend — To Make Changes to a Sales Order

ShortFall — To Run the ShortFall Generator

Recurring — Recall and Process Skeleton or Recurring Transactions

Intrastat — For Intrastat Dispatches Confirmation (SOP) window

Print — To Print a Sales Order

Labels — To Print Sales Order Labels

Reports — To Run Sales Order Reports

The Sales Order

Sales orders can be created for the products you supply and sent to customers by using the Enter option from the Sales Order Processing toolbar. Details from your Product records are automatically entered onto the Sales Orders whilst extra details can also be added, such as a delivery address, a customer order number for future reference or a settlement discount.

To create a Sales Order, click Modules, Sales Order Processing from the Sage 50 menu bar, then do the following:

1 Click New/Edit from the Sales Order Processing toolbar

2 Type required date if different and enter Customer Account Code, Customer details appear

103

Product Sales Order						
Details	Order Details	Footer Details	Payment Details	Despatched	Invoices	

Bobs Building Supplies
Timber Yard
123 Prescot Way
Alnwick
Northumberland
AL12 6GH

Type: Sales Order — Product Sales Order
Order No. <AutoNumber>
Date 11/10/2008 — Inv Ref
A/C BBS001 — Item No. Item 4 of 4

Product Code	Description	Quantity	Price £	Net £	V.A.T. £
CALC001	Calculator Desktop	1.00	9.50	9.50	1.67
REMEMBER01	Remember-Me Sticky Notes	20.00	2.85	57.00	9.72
PEN001	Ball Point Pen - Black	50.00	1.90	95.00	16.21
PEN004	Pencil HB	50.00	2.38	119.00	20.30

Deduction	Description	Net £		
Net Value Discount		0.00		

Total GBP £ 280.50 — 47.05
Carriage GBP £ 0.00 — 0.00
Gross GBP £ 328.35

Less Deposit GBP £ 0.00
Amount Due GBP £ 328.35

Save | Discard | Print | Complete | Cash Sales | Memorise | Recall | Close »

3 Enter the Product Code (use Finder button) and Quantity ordered

4 Repeat Step 3 for any additional products, then when finished click Save

5 Click Close

Hot tip

Use the Message box (i.e., the product code M) to add any text to the main body of the sales order, for example, 'goods supplied free'.

Hot tip

To include special one-off details against a sales item, click the Edit button from the Description box.

...cont'd

Beware

Once a Sales Order has been despatched in part or full, you cannot decrease the quantity of a product to less than the quantity despatched.

Don't forget

Sage 50 will generate an invoice and enter the Invoice Number for you automatically when the order is Despatched.

Hot tip

If you trade physical goods with Member States of the EU, use the Intrastat button for producing trade statistics. The supply of services is excluded. Intrastat replaced customs declarations as the source of trade statistics within the EU and is closely linked with the VAT system. Use the Sage F1 Help key for more information.

Sales Order Details

On the previous page you were shown how to create a Sales Order and save it immediately if no further details need to be entered. Sage 50, however, gives you the option to enter additional details about the order, such as where it should be delivered if different from the main address.

From the Sales Order window, do the following to enter additional order details:

1 Click on the Order Details tab

2 Enter Delivery Address (not yet set up) if required

3 Record any Notes here

4 Enter any relevant Customer Order Details, such as a Customer Order Number or a Due Despatch date

5 Click Save when finished

6 Click Close

Allocating Stock

Once a Sales Order has been created, stock needs allocating to it before any despatches can be recorded for the Order. Using the Allocate option from the Sales Order Processing toolbar automatically allocates the necessary stock needed for the selected Sales Order.

Sometimes there is insufficient stock available to complete an Order, in which case the Order will be marked as 'Part' complete. There may be times when you have enough stock, but wish to only send part of the Order. In this case you would use the Amend option to make changes to the Order. To allocate batched Sales Orders, do the following from within the Sales Order Processing window:

1 Click on the Sales Orders you wish to Allocate

2 Click Allocate from the toolbar

3 Click Yes to Confirm Allocation of stock

4 Note change in sales order Allocated status, then click Close

Hot tip

To view Sales Order details simply double-click on the item.

Don't forget

If Sage 50 cannot allocate all of the necessary stock to the order, a message box is displayed, giving suggestions and possible reasons why not.

105

Don't forget

If there is insufficient stock for a Sales Order, the Status 'Part' appears in the Sales Order Processing window. Fully allocated orders display a 'Full' status.

Despatching Sales Orders

Once stock is allocated to your sales orders, it can be despatched at any time. The Despatch option also updates the product records and creates a Product Invoice for the order, as well as printing a Delivery Note.

The product invoices created through Sales Order Processing appears in the Invoicing window. These invoices can be edited, but you cannot change the quantity of the product despatched. They can then be printed and posted to the sales and nominal ledgers in the same manner as invoices created using the Invoicing option.

Don't forget

If only part of an order is despatched, Sage 50 creates an invoice for that part. This means that when the order is fully despatched, there will be more than one invoice for it.

Hot tip

Use the Shortfall option to see if you have enough stock to fulfil orders or to place purchase orders if you do not.

106

1 From the Sales Order Processing window, select the required Sales Orders

2 Click Despatch from the toolbar

Don't forget

You can use the GDN button from the toolbar to quickly generate a Goods Delivery Note. Remember, though, that if you set up your GDN Options to 'Do not Generate', Sage 50 will not produce a goods despatch note and there will be no GDN option on the SOP toolbar.

3 Click Yes to print Delivery Notes, create Invoices and Update Stock

Confirm

Do you wish to create invoice details, update stock and record despatch for the selected order(s)?
To print a delivery note only click 'No'.

Yes | No | Cancel

4 Click Print Now for Delivery Notes

Confirm

Note - A Goods Despatched Note has been generated for this order and stored under the 'Despatched' tab of the order.
You can either print your delivery note now, or continue processing and print the Goods Despatched Note from the 'Despatched' tab of the order.

☐ Do not show this message again

Print Now | Print Later

5 Select Delivery Note layout, click Generate Report, then Print and Close

Amending & Printing Sales Orders

If you have allocated stock to a sales order, but have not yet despatched all of it, you can amend this allocation. This allows you to despatch a full order by reducing the stock allocation of another customer's order, hence perhaps reducing the number of customers waiting.

To amend the allocation of stock on a sales order

1 Select the Order from the Sales Order Processing window and click Amend

Amend Allocations

Bobs Building Supplies						
Timber Yard				Order Number	28	
123 Prescot Way				Order Date	13/10/2008	
Alnwick				Order Value	328.35	
Northumberland				Account Ref	BBS001	
AL12 6GH						

Product Code	Description	Ordered	Despatched	Outstanding	Allocated	This Despatch
CALC001	Calculator - Desktop	1.00	0.00	1.00	1.00	1.00
REMEMBER01	Remember-Me Stic...	20.00	0.00	20.00	10.00	10.00
PEN001	Ball Point Pen - Black	50.00	0.00	50.00	50.00	50.00
PEN004	Pencil - HB	50.00	0.00	50.00	50.00	50.00

Off Order | Allocate All | Despatch | Previous | Next | Close

2 Amend the Allocation as necessary

3 Click Close and note change in status from Full to Part

Printing Batched Orders

1 Select orders for printing and Click Print

2 Choose layout & click Generate Report

3 Click Print, then Close

Sales Order Printing

Description	File Name
11" Sales Order - Inc Line V.A.T. 8 Point	SALVAT11.layout
11" Sales Order - Inc Line V.A.T. 8 Point (Tax Breakdown)	TBSAVAT11.layout
11" Sales Order - No Line V.A.T. 10 Point	SALNEW11.layout
11" Sales Order - No Line V.A.T. 10 Point (Tax Breakdown)	TBSANT11.layout
A4 Sales Order - Inc Line V.A.T. 8 Point	SALVATA4.layout
A4 Sales Order - Inc Line V.A.T. 8 Point (Tax Breakdown)	TBSAVA4.layout
A4 Sales Order - No Line V.A.T. 10 Point	SALNEWA4.layout
A4 Sales Order - No Line V.A.T. 10 Point (Tax Breakdown)	TBSANA4.layout
e-Mail Sales Order	EMA_SOP.layout
e-Mail Sales Order (Tax Breakdown)	TBEMS.layout
Sales Order with BOM details (Including Special Items)	SOPBOM.layout

Generate Report | Preview
New | Edit | Delete | Close

Sales Orders Reports

Sage 50 provides you with a large variety of reports to help you run the Sales Order side of your business. For example, you have the facility to print a picking list for your warehouse from a particular order or the sales order shortage report to show you any shortfalls in the stock.

These reports are generated from the information entered when you created a sales order. To generate, for example, a Sales Order Picking List:

1 From the Sales Order Processing window, click Reports

2 Double-click folder & select required Layout

3 Click on Generate Report

4 Enter Criteria i.e. Sales Order number

5 Click OK to generate report

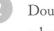

6 Click Print, then OK

9 Purchase Orders

Create and print Purchase Orders to send to your suppliers. You will be shown how to monitor orders raised and record deliveries received as well as produce reports to help track them.

The PO Processing Toolbar

From the POP toolbar you can create and print Purchase Orders as well as make amendments to orders you have already created. You have facilities for recording deliveries and producing useful reports about your Purchase Orders, such as a report indicating orders that have been delivered in part or full, or orders that are still outstanding.

New/Edit — To Create or View a Purchase Order

Order — To Put a Purchase Order 'on order'

Deliver — To Record Purchase Order Deliveries

GRN — To Complete a Goods Received Note

Amend — To Make Changes to a Purchase Order

Update — To Automatically Update the Purchase Ledger

Recurring — Recall and Process Skeleton or Recurring Transactions

Intrastat — For Intrastat Arrivals Confirmation (POP) window

Print — To Print a Purchase Order

Labels — To Print Purchase Order Labels

Reports — To Run Purchase Order Reports

Creating a Purchase Order

To record order details of any products you buy from a supplier, use the Enter option from the Purchase Order toolbar. Details entered straight onto the Purchase Order screen are taken directly from the product records for you by Sage 50.

You can also include additional details, such as delivery address or any settlement discount given to you by your supplier, to the order. To create a Purchase Order click POP from the Sage 50 toolbar then follow these steps:

1 Click New/Edit from the POP toolbar

2 Check date and enter Supplier Account Code

3 Supplier details appear here

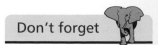

Don't forget

If a re-order quantity has been set up on the Product Record, this value is entered automatically for you in the Quantity field.

Don't forget

You can increase but not decrease the quantity for any Purchase Order you have already despatched, whether in full or part.

4 Enter the Product Code (use Finder button) & Quantity

5 Repeat Step 4 for additional products and click Save when finished

6 Click Close

Hot tip

For non-payment products use the product code M.

...cont'd

Entering Purchase Order Details

You may need to record further details on your Purchase Order, such as delivery details, carriage costs, settlement terms, supplier contact or the name of the person who took your order.

Sage 50 lets you do this through the Order Details or Footer Details tabs. From the Purchase Order window, do the following to enter additional order details:

1 Click on the Order Details tab

2 Enter Delivery Address if required

3 Record any Notes you wish to add here

To edit an existing purchase order simply double-click on it in the Purchase Order Processing window.

Hot tip

Save your Purchase Order as a Skeleton if you use these details regularly.

112

Product Purchase Order

Details | Order Details | Footer Details | Deliveries

Delivery Address

Wizard Training Limited
Wizard House
10 High Street
Anytown
Anyshire
AA1 2ZZ

Change...

Notes

Out of stock - 10 day lead time

DUNS Number

Supplier Order Details

Supplier Order No.
Supplier Tel. No.   0191 987 3897
Supplier Contact   Kathy Jordan
Order Taken By   MANAGER

Save | Discard | Print | Complete | Memorise | Recall | Send a Mail | Close | »

4 You can change who took the order here

5 Enter any relevant Supplier Order Details, such as an Order or Telephone Number

6 Click Save when all details have been entered

7 Click Close

Hot tip

Use the Footer Details tab to record any Carriage or Settlement terms and click the Deliveries tab to view delivery information.

Placing Orders 'on order'

Once a Purchase Order has been created, it has to be placed 'on order' before any deliveries can be recorded for it. The Sage 50 program then updates each product record with the new order details accordingly.

Use the Order option to automatically place a single or batch of Purchase Orders 'on order', as follows:

 1 From the Purchase Order Processing window, highlight all orders you wish to place 'on order' by clicking on them

2 Click on the Order button from the POP toolbar

Hot tip

Click the Search button to set up a filter to list only the orders you wish to work with.

Don't forget

To avoid costly mistakes, always check that the status of an order shows ON-ORDER after going through the process of placing it on order.

Purchase Order Processing (All Records)

New/Edit | Order | Deliver | GRN | Amend | Update | Recurring | Intrastat | Print | Labels | Reports

No.	Date	Name	Amount	On-Order	Delivered	Intrastat	Posted
20	30/07/2008	Superior Technologies Ltd	5504.11		COMPLETE		Y
21	01/08/2008	McNally Computer Supplies	1264.28		COMPLETE		Y
22	02/08/2008	Superior Technologies Ltd	3426.19		COMPLETE		Y
23	03/08/2008	Unique Systems	490.36		COMPLETE		Y
24	05/08/2008	Wiseman Paper Products	2317.52		COMPLETE		Y
25	05/08/2008	Concept Stationery Supplies	89.30		COMPLETE		Y
26	05/08/2008	McNally Computer Supplies	1012.13		COMPLETE		Y
27	05/08/2008	Superior Technologies Ltd	5304.68		COMPLETE		Y
28	05/08/2008	Wiseman Paper Products	383.50		COMPLETE		Y
29	28/08/2008	Wiseman Paper Products	1254.47		COMPLETE		Y
30	27/08/2008	Superior Technologies Ltd	102.20		COMPLETE		Y
31	29/08/2008	McNally Computer Supplies	3476.76		COMPLETE		Y
32	30/08/2008	Superior Technologies Ltd	331.87		COMPLETE		Y
33	27/08/2008	Concept Stationery Supplies	976.66		COMPLETE		Y
34	27/08/2008	McNally Computer Supplies	7922.79		COMPLETE		Y
35	27/09/2008	Unique Systems	150.40		COMPLETE		Y
36	27/08/2008	Wiseman Paper Products	1912.63		COMPLETE		Y
37	30/08/2008	McNally Computer Supplies	661.38		COMPLETE		
38	15/09/2008	McNally Computer Supplies	913.57	ON-ORDER			
39	23/10/2008	Wiseman Paper Products	720.63				
40	23/10/2008	Studio Designs	1381.34				

2 of 41 orders selected, total balance: 2101.97

Search | Swap | Clear | Delete | Print List | Duplicate | Close

Hot tip

You can also put Purchase Orders 'on order' from within the Amend Deliveries option.

3 Click No to print a copy of the Purchase Order later, else Yes to print now

Confirm
? Do you want to print the Purchase Orders for the selected items ?
Yes | No

4 Click Yes to place the selected items 'on order'

5 Note that items are now ON-ORDER, then click Close

Confirm
? Place all selected items On-Order ?
Yes | No

Recording Deliveries

To automatically record the complete delivery of stock for Purchase Orders use the Deliver option from the Purchase Order Processing toolbar.

You should remember that Sage 50 always assumes that you have taken full delivery of all the products needed to complete the selected Purchase Order. If a part delivery needs recording, you must do so using the Amend function (see page 116).

To record Purchase Order deliveries do the following:

Beware

When you use the Delivery option it is assumed that you have taken full delivery of all items on the Purchase Order. Note that the Delivery record cannot be altered later.

1 From the Purchase Order Processing window select any orders you wish to mark as Delivered

2 Click on Deliver from the POP toolbar

Don't forget

You can only record deliveries for orders which you have already put 'on order'.

Purchase Order Processing										(All Records)

New/Edit | Order | Deliver | GRN | Amend | Update | Recurring | Intrastat | Print | Labels | Reports

No.	Date	Name	Amount	On-Order	Delivered	Intrastat	Posted
21	01/08/2008	McNally Computer Supplies	1264.28		COMPLETE		Y
22	02/08/2008	Superior Technologies Ltd	3426.19		COMPLETE		Y
23	03/08/2008	Unique Systems	490.36		COMPLETE		Y
24	05/08/2008	Wiseman Paper Products	2317.52		COMPLETE		Y
25	05/08/2008	Concept Stationery Supplies	89.30		COMPLETE		Y
26	05/08/2008	McNally Computer Supplies	1812.13		COMPLETE		Y
27	05/08/2008	Superior Technologies Ltd	5304.68		COMPLETE		Y
28	05/08/2008	Wiseman Paper Products	383.50		COMPLETE		Y
29	28/08/2008	Wiseman Paper Products	1254.47		COMPLETE		Y
30	27/08/2008	Superior Technologies Ltd	102.20		COMPLETE		Y
31	29/08/2008	McNally Computer Supplies	3476.76		COMPLETE		Y
32	30/08/2008	Superior Technologies Ltd	331.87		COMPLETE		Y
33	27/08/2008	Concept Stationery Supplies	976.66		COMPLETE		Y
34	27/08/2008	McNally Computer Supplies	7922.79		COMPLETE		Y
35	27/08/2008	Unique Systems	150.40		COMPLETE		Y
36	27/08/2008	Wiseman Paper Products	1912.63		COMPLETE		Y
37	30/08/2008	McNally Computer Supplies	661.38		COMPLETE		
38	15/09/2008	McNally Computer Supplies	913.57	ON-ORDER			
39	23/10/2008	Wiseman Paper Products	720.63		COMPLETE		
40	23/10/2008	Studio Designs	1381.34	ON-ORDER	PART		
41	23/10/2008	Unique Systems	370.85				

1 of 41 orders selected, total balance: 913.57

Search | Swap | Clear | Delete | Print List | Duplicate | Close

Don't forget

Sage 50 automatically makes adjustments for each product that you mark as delivered.

3 Click Yes to Confirm delivery and update stock records, then choose whether to print a GRN now or later

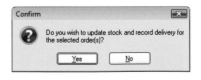

Confirm

Do you wish to update stock and record delivery for the selected order(s)?

Yes | No

4 Note the Purchase Order now displays as COMPLETE, then if finished click Close

Processing Purchases Manually

To check and keep track of your Purchase Orders use the Amend option. In this window you can manually place them 'on order' (thus updating On Order levels for the appropriate product records), record full or part deliveries of stock against each order and cancel orders.

Placing a Purchase Order 'on order' manually

You have already learned how to place Purchase Orders 'on order' using the Order button (Page 113). However, Sage 50 also allows you to do this manually as follows:

 From Purchase Order Processing window, select the purchase order you require

2 Click Amend to bring up the Amend Deliveries window

Product Code	Description	Project Ref	Cost Code	Ordered	Delivered	Outstanding	This Delivery
FIL002	Filing Cabinet - 5 ...			10.00	0.00	10.00	0.00
PEN006	Pencil - Chinagrap...			200.00	0.00	200.00	0.00

Order Number: 40
Order Date: 13/10/2008
Order Value: 1381.34
Account Ref: STU001

Studio Designs
7th Floor
Gilesgate House
7 Carlisle Road
Newcastle upon Tyne
NE1 4TF

3 Click on the Order button to place 'on order'

Product Code	Description	Project Ref	Cost Code	Ordered	Delivered	Outstanding	This Delivery
FIL002	Filing Cabinet - 5 ...			10.00	0.00	10.00	10.00
PEN006	Pencil - Chinagrap...			200.00	0.00	200.00	200.00

4 Note the order now looks normal and the full order quantity appears in This Delivery

5 Click Close

Hot tip

You can cancel a Purchase Order which is 'on order' using the Amend option. Just click Off Order to mark it as cancelled, click Order to put it back 'on order'.

Don't forget

You can use the GRN button from the toolbar to quickly generate a Goods Received Note. Remember, though, that if you set up your GRN Options in Invoice and Order Defaults to 'Do not Generate', Sage 50 will not produce a goods received note and no GRN option will appear on the POP toolbar.

Recording Deliveries Manually

You use the Deliver button from the Purchase Order Processing toolbar only when you have received full delivery of an order.

If you wish to record part deliveries, then you must use the Amend option, though you can still record full deliveries this way as well, should you need to. To record a Purchase Order part delivery, follow these steps:

1 From the Purchase Order Processing window select the order you wish to record a delivery for

2 Click on Amend from the POP toolbar

116

Amend Deliveries

Studio Designs
7th Floor
Gilesgate House
7 Carlisle Road
Newcastle upon Tyne
NE1 4TF

Order Number	40
Order Date	13/10/2008
Order Value	1381.34
Account Ref	STU001

Product Code	Description	Project Ref	Cost Code	Ordered	Delivered	Outstanding	This Delivery
FIL002	Filing Cabinet - 5 ...			10.00	0.00	10.00	5.00
PEN006	Pencil - Chinagrap...			200.00	0.00	200.00	200.00

Off Order   Deliver   Previous   Next   Close

3 Enter part quantity received in the This Delivery column

4 Click on the Deliver button to update your product record details

5 Click Yes to confirm updating of order

Confirm

Do you wish to update stock and record delivery for the selected order(s)?

Yes   No

6 Click Close to finish & note status is now PART delivered

Printing Batched Orders

Rather than print your Purchase Orders straight away you may have chosen to save them until later. This is useful if you only have one printer and need to change the stationery. When you are ready you can then print the orders out in batches.

As with all the printing facilities in Sage 50, you can send the Purchase Order direct to the printer, save it as a file or first preview it on the screen. To preview an order and then print it do the following:

 1 From the Purchase Order Processing window, select the order for printing

2 Click on Print from the POP toolbar

3 Select correct layout and ensure Preview is selected

4 Click Generate Report

5 On the preview, click Print then click OK

6 Click Close

Hot tip

Save time by emailing your Purchase Orders directly to your Suppliers.

Hot tip

To print a specific selection of Purchase Orders use the Search button facility.

Don't forget

If your business trades physical goods with Member States of the EU, use the Intrastat button for producing trade statistics.

Purchase Order Reports

Standard reports have already been set up for you to display any outstanding Purchase Orders, or orders which have already been delivered or part delivered. These reports can be previewed on screen, sent to your printer or saved to a file for previewing or printing later.

To generate a report of any Purchase Orders not yet delivered, do the following:

Hot tip

Make use of your Purchase Order Not Delivered or Part Delivered reports to track and monitor supplies.

1 From the Purchase Order Processing toolbar, click Reports

2 Select required layout and check Preview is selected

3 Click on Generate Report

4 Enter Criteria, if any applies

5 Click OK to generate report

Hot tip

Use the Outstanding Purchase Orders report regularly to help you keep track of orders still outstanding for delivery.

6 Click Print to send to printer, then OK & Close

118

10 Financials

Generate financial reports so you can analyse your business transactions. This includes the Trial Balance, Profit & Loss, the Balance Sheet, the Budget and Prior Year reports plus how to produce a VAT Return and make a submission online.

The Financials Toolbar

From this toolbar you can generate all the financial reports you need to not only keep track of how your business is doing financially but also trace back and find out when certain transactions took place. The Audit Trail is particularly useful as it is a complete record of your transaction activities, whilst the VAT function gives you all the features you need to produce accurate VAT Returns.

Audit

To Produce the Audit Trail

Trial

Run the Trial Balance Report

P and L

To Produce the Profit and Loss Report

Balance

To Produce the Balance Sheet Report

Ratio

Run the Quick Ratio Report

Variance

To Produce the Budget Report

Prior Yr

Run the Prior Year Report

VAT

To Produce a VAT Return

Verify

To Check for possible Audit or VAT Anomalies

Reports

To Run Financial Reports

The Audit Trail

The Audit Trail records details about transactions entered into the system and it is a very useful source of information for checking and cross referencing. It may also be referred to when auditing your accounts.

Sage 50 gives you a range of Audit Trail formats providing brief, summary or fully detailed reports which can be previewed, printed directly or saved as a file for use later. A report of deleted transactions can also be printed. Use the Audit Trail regularly to ensure your transactions are being recorded accurately.

To view the Audit Trail:

1 From the Sage 50 menu bar, click Modules then Financials to bring up the Financials window displaying the Audit Trail

Don't forget

Deleted transactions always appear in red.

Hot tip

Transaction codes used in the Audit Trail are explained on Page 49.

No	Type	Account	Nominal	Dept	Details	Date	Ref	Ex.Ref	Net	Ta
1203	BP	1200	7100	000	Rent Direct Debit	02/03/2008	DD/STO		1200.00	0.0
1204	BP	1200	2310	000	Hire Purchase Payment	28/03/2008	DD/STO		150.00	0.0
1205	BP	1200	7903	000	Hire Purchase Interest	28/03/2008	DD/STO		5.55	0.0
1206	BP	1200	7100	000	Rent Direct Debit	30/03/2008	DD/STO		1200.00	0.0
1207	BP	1200	7100	000	Rent Direct Debit	27/04/2008	DD/STO		1200.00	0.0
1208	BP	1200	2310	000	Hire Purchase Payment	28/04/2008	DD/STO		150.00	0.0
1209	BP	1200	7903	000	Hire Purchase Interest	28/04/2008	DD/STO		5.55	0.0
1210	BP	1200	7200	000	Electricity Direct Debit	01/05/2008	DD/STO		150.00	12.0
1211	BP	1200	7100	000	Rent Direct Debit	25/05/2008	DD/STO		1200.00	0.0
1212	BP	1200	2310	000	Hire Purchase Payment	28/05/2008	DD/STO		150.00	0.0
1213	BP	1200	7903	000	Hire Purchase Interest	28/05/2008	DD/STO		5.55	0.0
1214	BP	1200	7100	000	Rent Direct Debit	22/06/2008	DD/STO		1200.00	0.0
1215	BP	1200	2310	000	Hire Purchase Payment	28/06/2008	DD/STO		150.00	0.0
1216	BP	1200	7903	000	Hire Purchase Interest	28/06/2008	DD/STO		5.55	0.0
1217	BP	1200	7100	000	Rent Direct Debit	20/07/2008	DD/STO		1200.00	0.0
1218	BP	1200	2310	000	Hire Purchase Payment	28/07/2008	DD/STO		150.00	0.0
1219	BP	1200	7903	000	Hire Purchase Interest	28/07/2008	DD/STO		5.55	0.0
1220	BP	1200	2310	000	Hire Purchase Payment	28/08/2008	DD/STO		150.00	0.0
1221	BP	1200	7903	000	Hire Purchase Interest	28/08/2008	DD/STO		5.55	0.0
1222	SI	DUG001	4000	001	Whiteboard - Drywipe (1000 x 1500)	05/09/2008	74		3861.00	675.6
1223	SI	BRI001	4000	001	Calculator - Pocket	05/09/2008	75		294.00	50.1
1224	SI	PAT001	4000	001	JP030 Jet Printer	05/09/2008	76		902.50	153.9

Search   Find   Close

2 Use both horizontal and vertical arrow buttons and scroll bars to examine all transaction details

3 When you have finished examining the Audit Trail, click Close

Don't forget

When you clear transactions from the Audit Trail, Sage 50 brings them forward as opening balances in your financial reports.

...cont'd

To print the Audit Trail report

1 From the Financials toolbar click Audit

2 Select Audit Trail Type, e.g. Brief

3 Check Output is set to Preview and click Run to continue

4 Enter required Criteria

5 Click here to Exclude Deleted Transactions from the report

6 Click OK to produce the report

7 If you want to print the report, click Print & OK, then close all windows

The Trial Balance

This report displays a simple listing of the current balances in all your nominal ledger accounts. It shows total values for both the debit and credit entries for all the nominal codes containing a balance value.

Since Sage 50 controls the double-entry accounting for you, the debit and credit columns will always balance. To produce the Trial Balance report do the following:

1 From the Financials toolbar click Trial. This brings up the Print Output window

2 Ensure Preview is selected and click Run

3 Select period required here

4 Click OK to generate the Trial Balance

5 If you want to print the report, click Print & OK, then close all windows

Hot tip

You can run this report for any month as it proves a valuable source of data for management information.

123

Hot tip

When you open the Financials window, the display automatically jumps down to the bottom of the list so the most recently entered transaction is always highlighted first.

Print Output

Output

○ Printer
⊙ Preview
○ File
○ e-Mail

[Run] [Cancel]

Criteria

Criteria Values

Enter the values to use for the criteria in this report

| Period | To (inclusive) |

Preview a sample report for a specified number of records or transactions (0 for all) 0

[Help] [OK] [Cancel]

Period Trial Balance - Preview

Open | Export | Print | Page Setup | Printer Offsets | Email | Zoom In | Zoom Out | Close | Goto Page 1

Date: 11/10/2008   **Wizard Training Limited**   Page: 1
Time: 15:04:28   **Period Trial Balance**

To Period: Month 7, October 2008

N/C	Name	Debit	Credit
0020	Plant and Machinery	50,000.00	
0021	Plant/Machinery Depreciation		3,485.00
0040	Furniture and Fixtures	16,900.00	
0041	Furniture/Fixture Depreciation		93.00
0050	Motor Vehicles	20,300.00	
0051	Motor Vehicles Depreciation		2,091.92
1001	Stock	35,000.00	
1100	Debtors Control Account	91,924.24	
1200	Bank Current Account		8,529.20
1210	Bank Deposit Account	3,510.00	
1220	Building Society Account	507.53	
1230	Petty Cash	1,130.48	
1240	Company Credit Card	9,358.97	
2100	Creditors Control Account		36,341.21
2200	Sales Tax Control Account		23,141.66
2201	Purchase Tax Control Account	12,257.94	
2210	P.A.Y.E.		5,396.79
2211	National Insurance		2,006.98

Page 1 of 2   100%

Profit and Loss Report

This important financial report shows whether your business is trading at a profit over a particular period of time. The report can be produced for the current month or a range of consecutive months within your current financial year.

The balances of each of your income and expenditure nominal ledger accounts appear on the standard Profit and Loss report. These categories, i.e. Sales, Purchases, Direct Expenses and Overheads, are grouped together and display a sub-total. The Gross Profit/(Loss) and Net Profit/(Loss) amount is also shown.

Don't forget

Balances are posted before the start of the financial year and so will appear as a prior year adjustment on the balance sheet, not on the Profit and Loss Report sheet.

1. From the Financials window click P and L

2. Ensure Preview is selected and click Run

3. Select period required here

4. Select Default Layout of Accounts (1) then click OK

5. If you want to print the report, click Print & OK, then close all windows

Beware

Unless you have set up your own layout, ensure you choose the Default Layout of Accounts in Step 4, otherwise you will not generate the correct report.

The Balance Sheet

The Balance Sheet shows the financial position of a business at a particular time by outlining its assets (what it owns) and its liabilities (what it owes). There are two main types of assets, fixed and current. Fixed assets are long-term and have material substance such as, premises, equipment and vehicles; whilst current assets are continually changing and include stock, debtors, cash accounts, etc.

The Balance Sheet shows the fixed and current assets, as well as the liabilities. By adding together the assets and subtracting the liabilities, the Balance Sheet shows the Capital, or net assets.

1 Click Balance from the Financials toolbar

2 Select Preview & click Run

3 Select period required here

4 Select Default Layout of Accounts (1) then click OK

5 Click Print & OK, then close all windows

Hot tip

Use the Balance Sheet regularly to give a summary of your current financial position.

Don't forget

The difference between assets and liabilities is referred to as the company's net assets (or net worth).

125

Don't forget

Liabilities consist of both current and long-term. Current liabilities are amounts owing at the balance sheet date and due for repayment within 12 months or less, e.g. trade creditors. Long-term liabilities are amounts due for repayment in more than 12 months, e.g. a bank loan.

Print Output

Output
- ○ Printer
- ⊙ Preview
- ○ File
- ○ e-Mail

[Run] [Cancel]

Criteria Values

Enter the values to use for the criteria in this report

| Period | Between (inclusive) | 1, April 2008 | and | 7, October 2008 |
| Chart of Accounts | Is | 1: Default Layout of Ac |

Preview a sample report for a specified number of records or transactions (0 for all) 0

[Help] [OK] [Cancel]

Balance Sheet - Preview

Open | Export | Print | Page Setup | Printer Offsets | Email | Zoom In | Zoom Out | Close | Goto Page 1

Date: 11/10/2008   **Wizard Training Limited**   Page: 1
Time: 15:26:47   **Balance Sheet**

From: Month 1, April 2008
To: Month 7, October 2008
Chart of Account: Default Layout of Accounts

	Period	Year to Date
Fixed Assets		
Plant and Machinery	0.00	46,515.00
Furniture and Fixtures	0.00	16,807.00
Motor Vehicles	0.00	18,208.08
	0.00	81,530.08
Current Assets		
Stock	0.00	35,000.00
Debtors	4,536.68	91,924.24
Deposits and Cash	0.00	5,148.01
	4,536.68	132,072.25
Current Liabilities		
Creditors : Short Term	0.00	36,341.21
Taxation	0.00	7,403.77

Page 1 of 1   100%

Quick Ratio Report

Using the data available within the system, the Quick Ratio Report allows you to see the current liquidity position of the business. This type of information is necessary for making financial decisions about future investments or developments and will be required by a number of different parties, for example: management, bank managers, shareholders.

These Ratio Reports highlight both the strengths and the weaknesses in the financial position of your business. Credit and debit balances are compared to show the net balance using previously set up nominal account codes. You can edit the report to include other nominal accounts you wish to compare.

To view or edit the quick ratio report

1 From the Financials window, click Ratio

2 To edit the nominal accounts, use Finder button to select Nominal Code required

Hot tip

Use the Quick Ratio Report to see the immediate financial position of your company. This is useful when you are considering future investments etc.

Hot tip

Click the Save button to quickly store a handy Quick Ratio report for future reference.

N/C Ref	N/C Name	Debit	Credit
1100	Debtors Control Account	91924.24	0.00
1103	Prepayments	0.00	0.00
1200	Bank Current Account	0.00	8529.20
1210	Bank Deposit Account	3510.00	0.00
1220	Building Society Account	507.53	0.00
1230	Petty Cash	1130.48	0.00
1240	Company Credit Card	9358.97	0.00
2100	Creditors Control Account	0.00	36341.21
2109	Accruals	0.00	0.00
2200	Sales Tax Control Acco...	0.00	23141.66
2201	Purchase Tax Control A...	12257.94	0.00
3200	Profit and Loss Account	0.00	0.00
4000	Sales North	0.00	180619.53

129737.43

Save   Print   Delete   Close

3 Click Print, then Run in Print Output window

4 Select Period

5 Click OK

Criteria

Criteria Values

Period   To (inclusive)

Preview a sample report for a specified number of records or transactions (0 for all)   0

Help   OK   Cancel

The Budget Report

The Budget Report displays the current values in your purchases, sales, direct expenses and overhead account codes for the months you select and the year-to-date. Use this report to see how your business actually traded compared with the monthly budget you set against the nominal ledger accounts for the chosen months and the year-to-date.

1 Click Variance from the Financials toolbar

2 Ensure Preview is selected & click Run

3 In the Criteria box enter the From and To Period required

4 Select Default Layout of Accounts (1)

5 Click OK to generate the report

6 Click Print and OK, then colse all windows

127

Hot tip

You can amend your nominal account Budget values at any time by using the Global Changes feature from the Tools menu.

Hot tip

When you run a year end, Sage 50 offers you the option to move the actual monthly values for the year just ended to the budgets for the coming year. This sets the budget values to be what really happened in each month of the year just ended. You can also add a percentage increase to your budget values to reflect any anticipated rise in sales, purchases, costs, etc. for the coming year.

The VAT Return

For businesses that need to submit VAT Return forms to HM Revenue and Customs, Sage 50 provides all the features to enable you to do this quickly and accurately, calculating both input and output tax for you from the information you have entered over the period. This is a prime reason for keeping accurate accounts.

Hot tip

Use the Wizard button to guide you through the various stages of the VAT Return process.

Input tax is the VAT you are charged on your business purchases and expenses. Output tax is the VAT your business charges on its taxable supplies or services. Since Value Added Tax is a tax charged to the final consumer, a business needs to calculate what input tax can be reclaimed and how much output tax needs paying to Revenue and Customs. This is the purpose of the document called the VAT Return.

You have the facility to set up 100 tax codes, but on installation Sage 50 sets the standard UK and EC VAT rates for you, so you will probably not have to change anything. The default is set to the standard rate T1, presently at 17.5%, whilst others you may need are T0 (zero-rated) and T9 (transactions not involving VAT).

Don't forget

Before reconciling your VAT transactions, you should always back up your data files. Reconciling your transactions sets a flag against each transaction so it is automatically excluded from subsequent VAT Returns.

Within the nominal ledger there are three accounts, namely Sales Tax Control account (2200), Purchase Tax Control account (2201) and VAT liability account (2202). An accumulated total appears in the Sales account for the output tax charged to your customers whilst another accumulated total appears in the Purchase account for the input tax charged to your business.

When your VAT Return is due, enter the correct date range into the system and the program will calculate the difference between the input and output tax and will inform you of the net VAT due to either the Revenue and Customs or to yourselves.

Hot tip

The Audit Trail VAT column shows whether a transaction is reconciled or not:

- R = reconciled

- N = unreconciled

- a hyphen (-) or a dash (–) = a non-VAT transaction

After reconciling your VAT Return, VAT on the Sales and Purchases Control accounts for this VAT period need to be transferred to the VAT Liability nominal account. When a bank payment to the Revenue and Customs is made or received, the VAT Liability account is cleared, leaving a zero balance.

If you have Internet access, Sage 50 lets you make your VAT submission and payment online as detailed on Page 131, though you will first need to set up a Government Gateway Account. Sage Help on e-VAT shows you how to do this and has a link direct to the HMRC website.

To produce your VAT Return

1 From the Financials window click VAT to bring up the VAT Return window displaying zero totals

2 Enter the inclusive VAT period dates

3 Click Calculate to calculate totals for this return. You will be informed if any unreconciled transactions are found

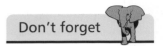

Don't forget

Ensure all transactions have been fully reconciled and the Audit Trail checked before running your VAT Return.

Hot tip

Use the Verify button to quickly run a series of basic checks to highlight possible Audit or VAT anomalies before running the VAT Return.

4 Click on a VAT total for a breakdown

5 Double-click on a Tax Code for a transaction breakdown

6 Close each window to return to VAT Return

7 Click Print, Run and OK

8 Click Reconcile & confirm

Hot tip

Three reports are available for printing: Detailed, Summary and the VAT Return. The Detailed and Summary reports give a breakdown of all the totals in each box on the VAT Return.

...cont'd

The VAT Transfer Wizard

Use the VAT Transfer Wizard to guide you through the transfer of your VAT liability once you have successfully reconciled and printed your VAT return.

1 From the Sage 50 menu, click Modules, select Wizards, then click VAT Transfer Wizard

2 Click Yes to confirm you wish to continue

VAT Transfer Wizard

VAT Transfer

Welcome to the VAT Liability Transfer Wizard.

Use the Wizard to guide you through the transfer of your VAT liability.

This Wizard should be used after you have successfully reconciled and printed your VAT return.

Cancel   Help   Back   Next   Finish

---

3 Click Next to proceed with the Wizard

4 Work through each screen entering details where required and clicking Next until Confirm Posting Details window

---

VAT Transfer Wizard

VAT Transfer

Confirm Posting Details

Confirm Posting details are correct.

Date	31/10/2008			
N / C	Description	Tc	Debit	Credit
2200	Sales Tax	T9	31441.67	
2202	VAT Liability	T9		31441.67
2201	Purchase Tax	T9		13755.10
2202	VAT Liability	T9	13755.10	

Cancel   Help   Back   Next   Finish

---

5 Click Finish to confirm details or Cancel to discard

e-VAT Submissions

From April 2010 at the earliest, all large and medium sized companies, most small traders and all newly registered VAT traders, will be required to file their VAT returns online and pay electronically.

If you didn't choose to enable e-VAT Submission during the setting of your VAT Preferences, you can do so later as follows:

1   Visit the HMRC website and obtain a Government Gateway Account

2   From Settings on the Sage 50 menu bar click Company Preferences

3   Click here to enable e-VAT Submissions

4   Enter your Credentials and Contact Details

5   Click OK to finish

Making an online VAT submission

1   From the Tasks List click Manage VAT

2   Choose the VAT Return required, click Submit Return and follow instructions

3   To pay online click Payment and follow the instructions

Don't forget

The Submit Return and HMRC Receipts buttons are only visible if you have Enabled e-Submissions in the Company Preferences VAT tab.

Don't forget

You can only make an online VAT submission for a return whose status is Pending or Partial. For a payment, the status must be Submitted but Not Paid.

Don't forget

To make VAT payments online make sure you have enabled e-Banking in the Bank defaults.

Financial Reports

Sage 50 offers a wide range of Financial Reports that provide management information to enable effective decision-making, planning and forecasting.

A considerable number of reports are set up at installation time, but many can be customised if required for your business by changing the appearance of the layout, the font type or by adding/removing certain text. Refer to Chapter 12 for more details. To generate a report do the following:

Don't forget

With Sage 50 you can calculate profit and loss for the current month or for any range of consecutive months within your current financial year.

1 From the Financials toolbar click Reports

2 Double-click folder and select the report layout required

Don't forget

The grouping and positioning of nominal codes on the Financial Reports are determined by the relevant Chart of Account in use.

3 Check Output is set to Preview

4 Click on Generate Report

5 Enter Criteria and click OK to generate the report, then Print

Don't forget

Information used for creating Financial Reports is taken from the actuals column in the Nominal Ledger Record.

To Verify System

1 Click Verify from Financials toolbar

2 Click OK to run checks

132

11 Fixed Assets

Learn all about Fixed Asset

Records and how to view

the value of all your assets.

The Fixed Assets Toolbar

This toolbar features options for creating Fixed Asset Records and setting up the method of depreciation, performing valuation of Fixed Assets and the generation of your Fixed Asset reports.

  Record   To Create a Fixed Asset Record

  Valuation   To Report on Asset Valuation

  Disposal   To Dispose a Fixed Asset

  Reports   To Run Fixed Asset Reports

Note:

In recent versions of Sage Accounts programs there is no Fixed Assets button on the navigation bar. Instead, do the following to bring up the Fixed Assets window:

1 On the Sage 50 menu bar, click Modules

2 Click on Fixed Assets Register to bring up the Fixed Assets window

Recording your Fixed Assets

Fixed Assets are items such as office equipment, buildings, machinery, etc. owned by the business. Their depreciation is an expense and can be offset against profits.

However, before recording Fixed Asset information, it is important that the correct method and rate of depreciation be decided upon and applied consistently. Different classes of Fixed Assets are often depreciated at different rates, for example, office furniture may be depreciated at a different rate to motor vehicles.

Sage 50 offers the choice of three depreciation methods: Straight Line, Reducing Balance and Write Off. For the Straight Line method, the asset is depreciated by a fixed percentage (calculated from the original Cost Price of the asset) every month until the asset is reduced to zero. For the Reducing Balance method, the asset is depreciated again monthly by a fixed percentage, but this time the percentage is applied to the new book value of the asset.

The last method, Write Off depreciation, makes one last posting to depreciate the remaining value of the asset.

When ready to enter your fixed assets for the first time you will notice that the Fixed Assets window is empty. As soon as Fixed Asset Records are entered, they will be displayed one record per line. To bring up the Fixed Assets window and view details:

1 From Modules, click Fixed Assets Register

2 Double-click on a record to view details

3 Click Close when done

Hot tip

Have the following information ready before entering your Fixed Asset Records; purchase date of asset and cost price, depreciation method and rate, depreciation balance sheet and depreciation profit & loss nominal codes.

135

Hot tip

To delete an Asset, just highlight it in the Fixed Assets window, then click the Delete button.

...cont'd

Adding Fixed Asset Records

The first time you use the Assets option, the Fixed Assets window will be empty. To add a Fixed Asset record, have all the necessary information to hand, then do the following:

Don't forget

You cannot save a new Fixed Asset record unless the nominal ledger posting details have all been entered.

1 From the Fixed Assets toolbar click Record

2 Enter a unique code to identify asset, no spaces allowed

3 Type a Description & a Serial Number, plus Location if relevant to this asset

Fixed Asset Record		
Details	Posting	

Asset Reference: W12ARD New Asset

Description: VW Golf TDi

Serial Number: W12ARD

Location/Employee: Garage

Date Purchased: 11/10/2008 Supplier A/C

Assets: 1 Directors Cars

Save Delete Discard Previous Next Close

Hot tip

Use the Tab key to move from one data entry box to the next.

4 Enter the Date Purchased

5 If the asset was bought from one of your current Suppliers, select Supplier A/C

6 For reporting purposes select Assets category from the list

Although you have now entered all the relevant details for this asset, before you can save this new record you still need to enter the appropriate nominal ledger posting details. This is explained on the next two pages.

Fixed Asset Depreciation

The Posting Tab in Fixed Asset Record window is used for entering the necessary nominal ledger posting details. Then, when you run the Month End/Year End depreciation posting routines, asset depreciation will be added to the appropriate account code as an expense to your business and will be shown on the Balance Sheet & Profit and Loss Report.

There are four depreciation accounts already set up in the Balance Sheet of the nominal ledger by Sage 50. Every time an asset is depreciated, the amount of depreciation is posted as a credit posting. Codes include 0021 (Plant/Machinery Depreciation), 0031 (Office Equipment Depreciation), 0041 (Furniture/Fixture Depreciation) and 0051 (Motor Vehicles Depreciation).

Similarly, four depreciation accounts are already set up for you in the Profit and Loss section of the nominal ledger. Every time an asset is depreciated, the value of that depreciation is added to the account code as an expense to the company (debit posting). Codes include 8001 (Plant/Machinery Depreciation), 8002 (Furniture/Fitting Depreciation), 8003 (Vehicle Depreciation) and 8004 (Office Equipment Depreciation).

You need to enter the annual rate of depreciation. For the Straight Line method, the value entered will be divided by twelve to calculate the monthly depreciation. For example, to depreciate an asset completely over five years using the straight line method, the Depreciation Rate would be 20%, depreciating at 1.666% monthly until after five years the book value is zero. So, for an item costing £15,000, a depreciation value of £250 would be posted for a term of 60 months.

Where Book Value details are required, then enter the current book value. If the asset is brand new, this should be the same as the Cost Price. If an asset has already been depreciated, then enter the cost price minus depreciation. If the reducing balance method was selected, the Book Value will be used to calculate the depreciation amount. Sage 50 will then automatically reduce this value by the depreciation amount when the month end procedure is run.

Don't forget

The Fixed Asset option does not post depreciation for you, only records the asset and current value. Use the Month End option to automatically make any depreciation postings.

Beware

Once you have saved a record, the depreciation method can only ever be changed to Write Off.

Hot tip

To record a Fixed Asset Disposal simply click on the Disposal button on the Fixed Assets toolbar and follow the step-by-step Wizard.

Depreciation and Valuation

Setting up a Fixed Asset depreciation posting

1 From the Fixed Asset Record select the Posting tab

2 Select Department where appropriate

3 Enter the nominal ledger Balance Sheet account code and the nominal ledger Profit & Loss account code

Fixed Asset Record

Details | Posting

Department	005

Balance Sheet Depreciation N/C	0051	P&L Depreciation	8003
Depreciation Method	Straight	Depreciation Rate	6.00
Cost Price	19550.00	Book Value	19550.00

Next Depreciation	97.75
Depreciation To Date	0.00
Date Last Posted	

Save | Delete | Discard | Previous | Next | Close

138

4 Select Depreciation Method & enter annual percentage Rate of Depreciation

5 Enter Cost Price (Net) & the current Book Value then click Save to store the details

Valuation of Fixed Assets

To see details about the current value of your assets including total cost, previous total depreciation and total current book value:

1 From the Fixed Assets window click Valuation to bring up the Asset Valuation window

2 When finished, click Close

12 The Report Designer

Layout a report, add filters, calculations and criteria.

The Report Designer

When you first install Sage 50, you can immediately generate and print all of the reports and stationery to suit most business needs. If you use stationery supplied by Sage, the data should fit in the pre-printed stationery forms without adjustment.

There will be occasions though when you need a new report not already supplied, or you need to modify an existing one to suit your specific needs. The Report Designer lets you do all of this to meet any specific requirements you may have.

The Report Designer included as an integral part of Sage 50 is actually a complete windows application on its own. The Designer has its own Title Bar, Menu Bar, and Desktop area on which you can open multiple document windows. Each document window can hold an entirely separate layout file, which means you can work on several layouts at once, if you wish. You can also convert your old Report Designer layouts to the new format. To run the new Report Designer do the following:

 1 On the Sage menu bar select Tools, then Report Designer

2 Double-click on a folder for a list of existing layouts

Hot tip

For more details about the Report Designer simply press F1.

Hot tip

Use the Report Designer to quickly create or modify your own reports, stationery layouts, letters and labels.

Creating a New Report

The following example shows you how to create a Customer Balance and Credit List for a single customer or a range of customers using the Report Wizard. The report contains the Customer's account reference, company name and account balance, together with their credit limit. The report is sorted to show the customer with the lowest balance first. The report also displays a balance total.

1 Click File, New from the Report Designer menu

2 Select Customer option and click Next

3 Double-click on a field table & select variable required from the list

4 Click Add ( ) to copy to Report Variables view

5 Repeat selection for all required variables & click Next

6 Click Next again as grouping not required

7 Select SALES_LEDGER.BALANCE for the Sort

8 Click Add, confirm Ascending & click Next

...cont'd

9 Select SALES_LEDGER.BALANCE from Totals

10 Click Remove (◄)

11 Click Next

Don't forget

Only numeric variables will be listed to total on when designing a report.

12 Remove all but Customer Ref & Transaction Date from the Selected criteria window

13 Click Finish to generate the report layout

Hot tip

Criteria Status can be set to Disabled, Enabled or Preset. This controls the Criteria screen that appears prior to running the report.

Hot tip

Should you ever need to remove all the Total Variables simply click the << Remove All button.

The Report Designer now generates the appropriate report layout for you. You will be able to see how the layout is divided into sections, i.e. Page Header, Details, Page Footer, etc. Remember though that depending upon your own options and settings, the initial layout may differ to that shown. For example, you may have to manually enable Crireria, add a Page Header or Footer, etc.

If the layout is not as required, you can modify the report later. First you need to check that it provides the information you require by running a report preview.

Previewing your Report

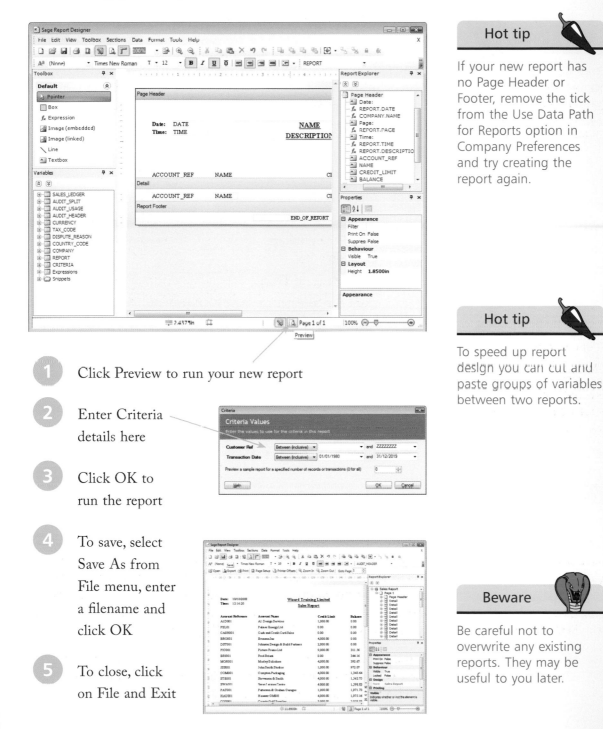

1 Click Preview to run your new report

2 Enter Criteria details here

3 Click OK to run the report

4 To save, select Save As from File menu, enter a filename and click OK

5 To close, click on File and Exit

Hot tip

If your new report has no Page Header or Footer, remove the tick from the Use Data Path for Reports option in Company Preferences and try creating the report again.

Hot tip

To speed up report design you can cut and paste groups of variables between two reports.

Beware

Be careful not to overwrite any existing reports. They may be useful to you later.

Modifying an Existing Report

The Report Designer lets you modify existing report layout files and default reports supplied with the program. These will, however, need saving under a new filename.

As an example, you can modify the report just created and saved to include only those customers having a balance greater than £1000. This is called a filter, which is embedded in the report layout. Assuming you saved your new report under Customers, to make this change it is easier to start from the Customers option:

1 From the Customer toolbar click on the Reports option

2 Open correct folder, select your report and click Edit

3 Click Data, Filters

144

4 Double-click SALES_LEDGER.CREDIT_LIMIT here

5 Type > and 1000 here, then OK

6 Click OK, Preview & Save

13 Opening Balances

This chapter explains how to enter opening balances for your customer, supplier, nominal and bank accounts as well as your products.

Hot tip

Print off a copy of the Opening Balances checklist from the F1 Help system to guide you during set up.

Don't forget

Posted Opening Balances for your customers and suppliers are displayed in the Trial Balance Report, which needs clearing before entering any Opening Balances for your nominal ledger accounts, bank accounts and products.

Hot tip

Note that these are the Nominal Codes used in the Trial Balance:

1100 = Debtors Control Account

2100 = Creditors Control Account

9998 = Suspense Account

Introduction

It is important to set up your opening balances correctly and in the right order. All accounts remain at zero until you enter opening balances for your Customers, Suppliers, Nominal, Bank and Products.

Where opening balances are carried forward, accurate figures need to be entered to reflect the true financial position of the business, for example, its Debtors, Creditors, Nominal Ledger Trial Balance, as well as its Stock.

Standard VAT and VAT Cash Accounting

Standard VAT calculates the VAT return on the invoices/credits you have raised for your customers or received from your suppliers, and any bank/cash payments or receipts or journal entries with vatable tax codes.

Customer opening balances can be entered as lump sum balances. It is recommended, however, that each outstanding invoice and credit note should be entered separately for cross referencing. Recording separate transactions will also provide accurate aged debtors analysis.

The second method, the VAT Cash Accounting scheme, is where the VAT return is calculated on the invoices/credits which you have received payment for from your customers or you have paid to your suppliers. It also includes any bank/cash payments or receipts or journal entries with vatable tax codes.

With VAT Cash Accounting each invoice and credit note must be entered for your customers individually, with the correct tax code.

The same Standard VAT and VAT Cash Accounting conditions apply for entering opening balances for suppliers. Again, it is recommended for Standard VAT that separate transactions be recorded for outstanding invoices and credit notes to match up with payments later instead of grouping them all together in one opening balance. Separate transactions will again provide accurate aged creditors information.

Standard VAT – O/B

With the Standard VAT accounting method opening balances can be entered as a lump sum or individual transactions. You set up your customer balances using the Customer Record, accessed by using the Customers button on the Sage 50 toolbar.

Where customer information exists already, you can refer to the Aged Debtors Analysis and Detailed Customer Activity reports for cross referencing purposes and for checking that opening balances are recorded accurately. The Aged Creditors and Detailed Supplier Activity reports are also available for your suppliers.

To enter customer Opening Balance details

1 From the Customers window click on the required record, then click Record on the toolbar

2 Click here to set up the Opening Balance

3 Enter invoice/credit note number, the original transaction date or last date of previous financial year, Type and Gross

4 Click Save to record details or Cancel to discard

147

Hot tip

Simply follow the same procedures as for Customers when entering opening balances for your Suppliers.

Hot tip

An Opening Balance can be entered as one total amount only if a detailed breakdown is not required.

Don't forget

T9 is set as the default non-vatable tax code.

VAT Cash Accounting – O/B

Using this particular scheme each customer invoice and credit note needs entering individually with the correct tax code because VAT is only considered when payment is being made. The opening balances can be entered using the Batch Invoices or Credits screens.

To enter customer Opening Balance details

1 From the Customers window click on the required record, then click Record on the toolbar

2 Click here to set up the Opening Balance

3 Enter invoice/credit note number

4 Enter invoice/credit note number, the original transaction date or last date of previous financial year and Type

5 Enter Net amount. If you want to enter a single opening balance, enter total net amount of all invoices here

6 Tax Code and VAT are entered for you. Check, then click Save

Hot tip

To quickly identify reference numbers use the Audit Trail from within Financials.

Hot tip

Enter the original date of the invoice or credit note for accurate aged debtors analysis or last date of the previous financial year.

Don't forget

The default tax code and VAT appear automatically, but can be changed as necessary.

Clearing Opening Balances

When opening balances for your customers and suppliers are saved, they are posted to the Trial Balance. These entries need clearing or they will be duplicated when posting opening balances for your nominal ledger accounts. This will produce an incorrect Balance Sheet.

Before you start, make a note from your Trial Balance of the values of your Debtors and Creditors Control Accounts, your Sales Tax and Purchase Tax Control Accounts and your Suspense Account and whether each one is a debit or a credit, for example:

Trial Balance

Name	TC	Debit	Credit
Debtors Control Account	T9	30,687.19	
Creditors Control Account	T9		21,189.78
Suspense	T9		9,497.41
BALANCE		30,687.19	30,687.19

Once the relevant details have been noted, a Journal Entry from the Nominal Ledger needs to be made to clear the balances. Using the details from the above example, the entry would be as follows:

Journal Entry

Name	TC	Debit	Credit
Debtors Control Account	T9		30,687.19
Creditors Control Account	T9	21,189.78	
Suspense	T9	9,497.41	
BALANCE		30,687.19	30,687.19

Don't forget

Remember to print a copy of your Trial Balance Report BEFORE clearing the opening balances.

Hot tip

When entering journal entries into the transaction table, use opposite values from the Trial Balance, i.e. Debit (+) and Credit (-).

Beware

The journal entry can only be saved when the value in the Balance box is zero.

...cont'd

Once you have noted what entries you need to make, you can add them to the Journal. When you process these entries, the opening balances in the Trial Balance will be cleared. To make the entries do the following:

1 From the menu bar click Modules, then Nominal Ledger

2 Click on Journals from the Nominal Ledger window

3 The Reference entry is optional. Type a reference if desired then check for correct Date

4 Enter details for both the credit and debits

Beware

Always bear in mind that for a journal entry, the VAT is neither calculated nor posted for you to the VAT control account record. You have to do this manually.

150

N/C	Name	Dept	Details	T/C	Debit	Credit
1100	Debtors Control Account	000	Clear O/B	T9	0.00	30687.19
2100	Creditors Control Account	000	Clear O/B	T9	21189.78	0.00
9998	Suspense Account	000	Clear O/B	T9	9497.41	0.00
					0.00	0.00

Reference: CLEAROB Posting Date: 11/10/2008 Balance: 0.00

Totals: 30687.19 30687.19

Save Discard Memorise Recall Print List Close

5 Note, the default Tax code of T9 is entered for you by Sage 50

6 Check total Debit and Credit are equal and a zero balance is displayed in the Balance box

7 Click Save to process your journal or Discard to cancel

8 Click Close to return to Nominal Ledger window

Hot tip

If you make a mistake just click on the Discard button and start again.

Entering Balances Mid-Year

Sage 50 needs Opening Balances in order to produce accurate financial statements. Since all accounts in all the ledgers have a zero balance when the program is first installed, it is important that the Opening Balances are entered as soon as possible. Without them your financial statements will not be up to date and accurate.

It is, however, quite possible to start using Sage 50 at any time through your financial year, and then enter the Opening Balances as they become available. For instance, if you have been in business for some time you will already have stock, products, customers and suppliers. You will have a transaction history. When you first start to use Sage 50 you will set up Records for your Customers, Suppliers, Products etc. This is when you can start to enter some Opening Balances.

If you do start to use Sage 50 part way through your financial year, you should contact your accountant as soon as possible for a detailed list showing all your outstanding Debtors and Creditors. You can then use this as the Opening Balances for your Customers and Suppliers.

You also need to ask for a Trial Balance from your accountant, which will give you the Opening Balances for each Nominal Ledger and Bank account.

You must at all times make sure that the information you enter is accurate. If you need to enter Opening Balances part way through your financial year, you will probably have a lot of Nominal Ledger opening balances to enter as well! It is important, therefore, that you enter these accurately otherwise your balance sheet will be incorrect.

You will also need to enter any year-to-date values from your Profit and Loss accounts. Your accountant should be able to provide you with this.

Hot tip

When you start using Sage 50 for the first time and you set up Product records, this is also a good time to have a stock take so that you know the details you are entering are accurate. Sage 50 can only produce accurate reports if the information you enter is correct. This is also a good time to check that Customer and Supplier details are still up-to-date.

151

Don't forget

If you do not enter a Cost Price in the Opening Product Setup box, then the product code is recorded as zero. This could affect your finance reports later.

Nominal Ledger & Bank A/c

When entering opening balances for your Nominal Ledger or Bank account, double-entry postings are applied by Sage 50. For example, if you post a debit opening balance of £1,000 to your Building Society account (1220 by default), Sage 50 will automatically post £1,000 as a credit to your Suspense Account (9998 by default).

After you have entered all your Nominal Ledger and Bank account opening balances, the balance of the Suspense Account should be zero again. A new Trial Balance needs to be printed to check that opening balances have been included for all your nominal accounts. If you still have a balance in your Suspense Account (i.e. it is not zero), an opening balance may have been omitted or a debit or credit misposted.

Nominal ledger opening balances

1. From the menu bar click Modules, then Nominal Ledger

2. Select the required account & click on the Record button

3. Click the O/B button to enter the balance

4. Enter opening balance details

5. Click Save then Close

Don't forget

If you have money in the bank or building society, their statement shows you have a balance under the credit column. They owe you that money, you are the creditor. When this money is recorded in your accounts, such asset balances are recorded the opposite way round as debits. If you have money in your bank or building society, the balance must be entered as a debit.

Hot tip

Enter an opening balance for each nominal account that appears on your Trial Balance.

Bank Opening Balances

You can also set up a Bank account Opening Balance directly
from the Bank Record. To do this follow these steps:

1 From the Sage 50 menu bar click Modules, then Bank

2 Click on the Bank Record you wish to set up an Opening
Balance for and click on Record

3 Click the O/B button

Hot tip

An asset should always
have a debit entry, whilst
a liability should always
have a credit entry.

4 Enter Date if different.
Then enter the opening
balance as a Receipt
or Payment. If you
have money in your
bank, this will be
a Receipt

Opening Balance Setup	
Ref	O/Bal
Date	11/10/2008
Receipt GBP £	1000.00
Payment GBP £	0.00
	Save Cancel

Hot tip

If you have money in
your bank account,
i.e. a debit, enter it as
a Receipt. If you are
overdrawn, i.e. a credit,
enter it as a Payment.

5 Click Save to record
the Opening balance
information, then close the Bank record

Product Opening Balances

When you create a Product Record, you will probably enter an Opening Balance for that product if you already have some in stock. However, there will be times when you need to enter an Opening Balance at a later date to that when the Record was first set up.

If you do the latter, when you save the Opening Balance for a product, Sage 50 posts an Adjustment In transaction, which appears on the product reports. The valuation report will show the opening stock quantity at the cost price entered. To set up a Product Opening Balance:

Don't forget

If you have selected the Ignore Stock Levels check box, you will not be able to enter an opening balance for this product.

1 From the Sage 50 menu bar click Modules, then Products

2 Select the Product requiring an opening balance

3 Click Record, then click O/B button on the In Stock box

Hot tip

To store a JPEG image of the item with the stock record just select the Web tab then click on the Add button in the Image section.

154

Product Record - FX030 Multifunctional Fax								

Details | Memo | BOM | Sales | Graph | Activity | Discount | Web

Product Details

Product Code: FAX003 Item Type: Stock Item
Description: FX030 Multifunctional Fax
Category: 9 Telecomunications
IntraStat Com. Code: Location: Supplied Direct
Com. Code Description: Weight (kg): 0.00

Ordering

Last Cost Price (Standard): 360.00
Last Cost Price (Discounted): 360.00
Last Ord Qty: 0.00
Last Ord Date:

Defaults

Sales Nominal Code: 4000 Tax Code: T1 17.50
Purchase Nominal Code: 5000 Part No.: 000006872
Supplier A/C: WAL001 Department: 001

Sales Price

Price: 460.00
Unit of Sale: Each
Pricing Structure

Status

In Stock: 0.00 Free Stock: 0.00 Re-order Level: 0.00
Allocated: 0.00 On Order: 0.00 Re-order Qty: 0.00

Stock Take

Date: / /
Quantity: 0.00

Save | Discard | Delete | Previous | Next | Print List | Close

Don't forget

Remember to enter the Cost Price for the Product when you set up the Opening Balance.

4 Enter Opening Balance details here

5 Click Save to return to the Products Record, then Close

Opening Product Setup			
Ref	Date	Quantity	Cost Price
O/BAL	11/10/2008	20.00	0.00

Save | Cancel

14 Data Management

This chapter shows you important routines and procedures you need to use regularly to maintain your data integrity. Backing up of data is the most important as problems could occur at any time.

Backing Up Data

Regular data backup (at least once daily) is essential in case of system error, when valuable data can be corrupted and sometimes lost. If this happens, you can at least restore important data files, reports and/or layout templates from your most up-to-date backup. A backup routine is provided by Sage 50 that remembers which drive or location you last used, but this can be changed to save to any drive and/or directory you require.

Backing up procedures vary from business to business; some use five disks for Monday to Friday and repeat their usage the following week. The important thing is to backup your data at least once a day! Sage 50 always prompts you to back up when you Exit the program, but to perform a backup at any other time, do the following:

Always keep your backups in a safe and secure place.

1 From the Sage 50 menu, click on File, then Backup

2 Click No, unless you first want to check your data

Although you are given the option of checking your data before doing a backup, it is advisable to click No and take the backup first, just in case errors are detected and you need copies of the data. Then take a final backup, this time running the data check procedure, if required.

3 To backup using the default Filename choose a Location and click OK; else to make changes follow Steps 4–5

4 To choose which File Types to backup use Advanced Options tab

5 Click OK

Restoring Data

Hopefully you should never have to restore your files, but should you be unlucky and suffer data loss or corruption, the Restore procedure allows you to revert to a previous backup. The backup you use to restore data is up to you, but it will normally be the most recent.

The Restore facility allows data from your backup disks to replace your old data by erasing it and starting again. It is, therefore, very important to correctly label disks when you take a backup, and always keep them in a safe place. You may even consider keeping a second copy somewhere other than on the premises in case of fire or theft!

Since the restore procedure erases your old data, any data you entered after the last backup is lost and will need to be entered again, so ensure you take frequent backups. Make sure that the Restore is first necessary, then do the following:

1 From the Sage 50 menu click on File, then Restore

2 Click OK to restore data files from default drive, else go to Step 3

3 If you are restoring from a different drive, enter location here

4 Click OK

5 Click OK to confirm and perform the data restore

File	Edit	View	Modules

New ▶
Open ▶
Close   Ctrl+F4
Backup...
Import...
Maintenance...
Restore...
Send ▶
Log Off
Exit

157

Hot tip

It is always advisable to run the Check Data option from File, Maintenance after you have restored your data.

Beware

Restoring data will completely erase your current Sage 50 data and replace it with data from your backup disks.

Don't forget

If you cancel whilst performing a Restore, Sage requires you to log in again.

Changing Global Values

There are certain values in Sage 50, such as Credit Limits, that have applications throughout the program. From time to time certain record values may need changing for all your records or for a selected group. To save time, these values can be changed quickly and easily by using the Global Changes Wizard. The Wizard guides you with on-screen instructions to make the necessary changes where required.

Values within the customer, supplier and nominal ledger records can be changed as well as certain values within your product records, for example the product sales price could be increased globally by 5% or the re-order level increased for a range of products. To run the Wizard:

Hot tip

Use the Global Changes option to alter the values for either all or for a selected group of accounts or products.

1. From the Sage 50 menu, select Tools

2. Click on Global Changes to start the Wizard, then click Next to continue

3. Select the area where you want to make a Global Change

4. Click Next to continue

Don't forget

Remember that you can also use the Global Changes Wizard to quickly set up customer turnover and credit limits, supplier turnover and credit limits, and nominal budgets.

5. Select items to apply change to

6. Click Next to continue

7 Select type of change and enter a value before progressing

8 Click Next to continue

9 Check correct items are to be processed

10 Click Next to continue

11 Check that the details are correct. If you need to make any changes, use the Back button until you get to the appropriate screen, make the changes, then keep clicking Next to get back to this screen

12 Click Finish to action the changes

Whilst the Global Changes Wizard allows you to make changes quickly and easily, be very careful when using it and always double-check your values because when you click Finish, the changes you have entered are actioned immediately. In some cases these are quite major changes, such as increasing all product sales prices by a stated percentage. If you were to accidentally enter the wrong percentage, you cannot easily undo the resulting changes!

Hot tip

To exit from a wizard at any point, choose the Cancel button or press ALT + F4.

Beware

Also use the Global Changes Wizard to set up product sales and purchase prices, Discount Rates, Re-order Levels and Re-order Quantities for your Products.

Beware

Always check you have entered the correct information as you may not be able to easily undo changes.

159

Importing Data

It can be very laborious entering a lot of data into certain records so Sage 50 lets you import data into the following record types – customers, suppliers, products and nominal ledger – provided, of course, it conforms to the correct file format. A group of new records can be created and imported directly into Sage 50 or existing records updated with new details, replacing records being entered individually.

The text can be easily produced using any program which allows you to save the file in text format (.txt), for example, a word processing, spreadsheet or accounts package. The text must be in a specific format otherwise it will not be imported correctly and errors will be reported. These files are called CSV files (Comma Separated Values).

The following rules apply:

- A comma separates each unit of data, i.e. B01,Bolt,100,0.2

- Each data record takes up a single line

- Each data record is terminated by pressing ENTER

- Any spaces at the start or end of a data unit are ignored, but spaces within data units are included

- Use quotes to include commas within a data unit, i.e. "25, Bell Lane"

- Each data unit in a record must be entered in strict order to avoid being imported incorrectly

- Two consecutive commas (,,) forces a move to the next data unit

An example of three typical CSV data records:

1,SI,BROWN,4000,2,Supplies,03/10/08,,27.15,T1,Y

2,SC,WHITE,4000,2,Credit,14/10/08,,35.00,T1,N

3,PI,BLACK,5000,4,Equipment,25/11/08,,52.50,T1,Y

Beware

Avoid import errors by not exceeding maximum data unit length and using the correct data type, e.g. do not enter a decimal number into a integer data unit.

Don't forget

When importing account code data of customers and suppliers records, it is converted to upper-case and restricted to eight characters. Blank spaces are removed.

To Import a Data File

1   From the Sage 50
     menu select File, then
     click Import

2   Click on correct
     Import Type here

161

3   Click Run to continue

4   Select Drive or Directory to Import from

5   Enter Name of File to Import or select from list

6   Click Open

File Maintenance

Sage 50 provides five important options to manage and check the validity of your data files. These features include checking for input errors, allowing manual data error corrections, data compression, re-indexing and building new data files.

Error Checking

You should use the Check Data facility to check the validity of your data files. If necessary you can then make corrections where required. This facility needs to be run regularly, when making backups and after restoring data.

Hot tip

Use the Check Data option on a daily basis to check for errors, so they can be quickly detected and rectified.

Don't forget

If there are problems whilst checking the data, a File Maintenance Problem Report dialog box appears which includes a Summary and details of Comments, Errors or Warnings.

162

Hot tip

To print out an error report, select the category tab required from the File Maintenance Problems Report dialog box and click the Print button.

1 From the Sage 50 menu select File, then click on Maintenance

2 From the File maintenance window click Check Data

3 Checking Data Files box shows the progress

4 Check out the details using Tabs

5 Click Fix to correct errors, else Close

Correcting Transactions

Any mistakes made while entering transactions can be corrected using the Corrections option from the File Maintenance window. These transactions, however, can only be edited or deleted if they are still held in the Audit Trail. To correct a transaction:

 Click Corrections from the File Maintenance window

 Select transaction to correct

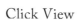

3 Click View

4 For changes to the customer/supplier account, details, reference or date, make your corrections here

163

5 For more changes click View

6 To change the nominal account, details, department, amount or VAT amount/code, make your corrections here

7 Close and Save

...cont'd

Reversing VAT Reconciled Transactions

You can delete a transaction provided it has not already been reconciled on the VAT Return. However, any VAT reconciled transaction will display a Reverse button instead of the Delete button in the Transaction Record window. To reverse VAT reconciliation on a transaction:

1 From the Posting Error Corrections window, select transaction and click View

2 To reverse VAT reconciliation click on the Reverse button

3 Click Yes to confirm

Data Compression

When there has been a lot of activity, such as deletion or amendments of any records, use the Compress Data option to produce a new set of data files. Sage 50 will then reduce file size by removing these deleted records, freeing up disk space. To perform data compression, do this:

1 Click Compress Data from the File Maintenance Box

2 Click Compress

3 Click Close

Rebuild

This Sage 50 option is for creating a new or selected set of data files. From the File Maintenance window:

1 Click Rebuild

2 Select files and click OK

Write Off, Refund & Return

Use these options to carry out accounting procedures that affect your customer and supplier accounts, e.g. cheque returns, invoice refunds and outstanding invoice transactions. The way you record these depends on your VAT method.

Refunds

Use this facility for credit notes, payments on account and invoices where a money refund is required rather than a replacement of goods or provision of services. If you are using the Standard VAT Scheme, do the following:

1 From the Suppliers Tasks list select Write Off/Refund

2 Select where you want to make the amendments

3 Click Next

4 Select the account to whom the invoice refund is to be made

5 Click Next to Continue

Don't forget

Sage 50 procedures for these functions vary depending on whether you are using the Standard VAT Scheme or VAT Cash Accounting.

Hot tip

For VAT Cash Accounting the transaction needs writing off manually. For more information, refer to Recording Refunds (VAT Cash Accounting) section of the Sage Help.

165

Hot tip

To find out if you are able to reclaim VAT paid on a Write Off, call HM Revenue and Customs.

...cont'd

Beware

Remember that this option is NOT suitable for anyone using VAT Cash Accounting as it does not adjust the VAT value for you.

Hot tip

If the presented summary of information is incorrect, simply use the Back button to return to the appropriate box and modify.

6 Select the invoice being refunded

7 Click Next to continue

8 Select the bank account you wish to post to

9 Click Next

10 Enter the correct date to use for the transaction

11 Click Next

12 A summary now appears

13 Check carefully that it is all correct. Use the Back button if you need to make any change, else go to Step 14

14 Click Finish to post changes to your ledgers

Write Off

At times a customer will not or cannot pay an outstanding debt, so the amount has to be written off to a bad debt account. The steps are very similar to a Refund, but fewer. Just select the appropriate Write Off for Step 2 on Page 165 and follow the simple instructions.

Cheque Returns

Occasionally, you may need to record a cheque from a customer that you wish to cancel or that the bank has returned. If you use the Standard VAT Scheme, do this:

 1 From the Customers Tasks list select Write Off/Refund

2 Click Customer Cheque Returns and Next

3 Select account, and click Next

4 Select the cheque and carry out Steps 9–14 on Page 166

Don't forget

Using a credit note to refund an outstanding customer invoice is known as allocating the credit note to the customer invoice.

Don't forget

When a sales credit note is posted to the customer's account it assumes the same reference as the refunded invoice.

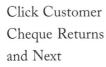

Don't forget

To record a refund using the Write Off, Refunds and Returns Wizard, the refund must need to be fully refunded and must not have been removed from the Audit Trail. If it has been removed or you need to make a partial refund, you must use the manual refund method.

167

Posting Contra Entries

Where you have a customer who is also one of your suppliers, you may offset sales invoices against your supplier's purchase invoices. To do this, you use the Contra Entries option from the Tools menu to match one or more sales invoices with your purchase invoices. Sage 50 will then automatically update the appropriate ledgers. To post a Contra Entry:

Don't forget

If VAT Cash Accounting is being used, make sure the selected transactions have matching tax codes.

1 From the Sage 50 menu click Tools

2 Click on Contra Entries to bring up the Contra Entries window

3 Select Customer (Sales Ledger) and Supplier (Purchase Ledger) accounts

Don't forget

You cannot amend any of the values shown in the Total boxes.

Hot tip

If your totals do not match, a warning message appears asking whether you want to make part-Contra Entries for the lowest amount. If acceptable click the Yes button or No to cancel the Contra Entries.

4 Select outstanding invoice (on sales side) from the list

5 Select invoice to apply Contra Entry for

6 Click OK to finish

Run Period End Functions

Period End options are essential monthly and year end procedures for updating the accounting system. For example, for posting accruals, prepayments and depreciation. The Audit Trail can then be cleared of any unwanted transactions whilst stock can be cleared from your Product history if you so wish.

Through running these procedures, you will also be preparing Sage 50 so that you are ready to enter transactions when you move into a new financial period.

Month End

At each month end it is important to post your prepayments, accruals and depreciation values. Sage 50 will process these transactions automatically and update your nominal account records and Audit Trail for you. The option also exists to clear down your month to date turnover figures for your customer and supplier records.

Once you have run the Month End procedures, this is an opportune time to produce some of your financial reports, for example, the Profit and Loss, Balance Sheet, Trial Balance, Budget and Prior Year Analysis reports. Customer statements and Aged analysis reports for Debtors and Creditors will also prove useful.

Month End Guidelines

Here is a check list for the Month End:

- Check all relevant transactions have been posted

- Check recurring entries have been set up and processed

- Check prepayments, accruals and depreciation have been set up

- Complete your bank reconciliation

- Print product history, valuation and profit reports

- Post product journals for your Profit and Loss & Balance Sheet

If program date needs changing for Month End procedure, select Change Program Date from the Settings menu. Remember to re-set the date back to the correct date when done.

Backup your data files before and after running Month End procedures.

Use File Maintenance Check and Compress Data options to check your files.

...cont'd

After following the Month End guidelines it is time to run the month end procedure. You will probably want to run it on a day other than the actual last calendar day of the month, as this is often more convenient. You will therefore have to change the program date first. To do this, simply follow these steps:

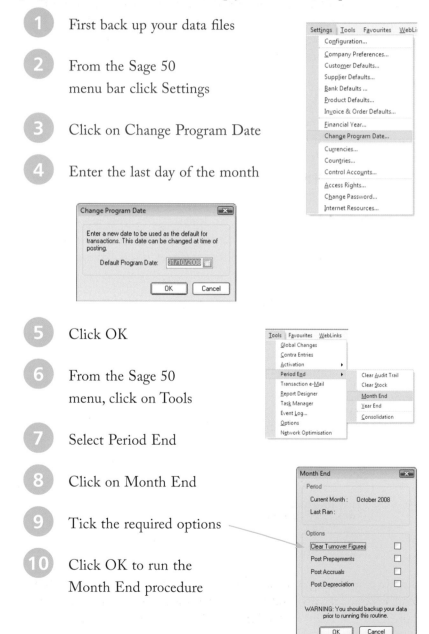

1. First back up your data files

2. From the Sage 50 menu bar click Settings

3. Click on Change Program Date

4. Enter the last day of the month

5. Click OK

6. From the Sage 50 menu, click on Tools

7. Select Period End

8. Click on Month End

9. Tick the required options

10. Click OK to run the Month End procedure

Year End

Before you run the Year End, Month End procedures must be completed, together with any final adjustments.

First, when you run Month End on the last month of the current financial year, DO NOT clear the Audit Trail. Once values for the month end have been checked and you are satisfied that they are correct, set the program date to the last date of the current financial year and run Year End:

1   Set the program date to the last day of the financial year by doing Steps 1–5 on Page 170

2   From the Sage 50 menu, click on Tools

3   Select Period End

4   Click on Year End

5   Select here to update your budget figures for each nominal ledger profit and loss account and each product record with the actual values from the year just ending

6   Change Year End Journals Date if necessary

7   Select Output

8   Click OK to run

Lastly, remove any unwanted Customer, Supplier, Nominal, Bank and Product records and reset system date. You are now ready to continue entering transactions for the new financial year.

Hot tip

Take at least two backups of your data files both before and after running the Year End routine.

Beware

After Year End check your Financial Year Start Date before entering any new transactions.

171

Beware

You must not consolidate companies that have different base currencies.

Clearing Audit Trail and Stock

This option lets you remove paid and reconciled transactions prior to a specified date from the Audit Trail. This makes the ledgers easier to read. Reconciled transactions on the nominal ledger are brought forward as opening balances.

Sage 50 can store up to 2,000,000,000 transactions in the Audit Trail, so transactions do not have to be removed, but by deleting unwanted transactions, it will free disk space and provide faster access to information.

Don't forget

Only paid, allocated and reconciled transactions are removed from the Audit Trail.

Don't forget

Before running the Clear Stock option, you should back up your data and print your stock valuation and stock history reports. Do likewise before clearing the Audit Trail.

172

Beware

Departmental reporting and activity will be affected by removing transactions from the Audit Trail.

1. From the Tools menu, select Period End, click Clear Audit Trail, then Next on the first two prompt screens

2. Enter required date

3. Click Next, then Process to clear the Audit Trail

Clear Stock

This option can be run as part of the Month End and Year End procedures. It allows you to decide when to clear transactions from your Product History.

1. From the Tools menu, select Period End, then click Clear Stock

2. Click Yes to continue

3. Enter date here

4. Click OK

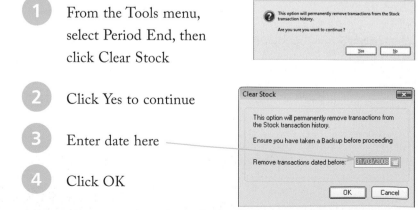

15 The Task Manager

This chapter shows you how to use the Task Manager for setting up useful functions such as a reminder list of tasks to do, i.e. bills to pay, people to contact, etc. It also lets you quickly view the status of your accounts, invoices, sales orders and purchase orders as well as check how much you owe and vice versa.

Features of the Tasks Option

Use the Tasks option to set up a list of jobs that you need to do and to prompt you of any tasks that are currently due, overdue or recently completed. By setting up these tasks it acts as a reminder of the actions you need to take to run your business efficiently, produces important information and saves valuable time.

You can use the Tasks option to help you:

- Set up a list of tasks that you need to do and also view any tasks that are either completed, due or overdue

- List people you need to contact today or in the future, or record and view any contacts that you have 'completed' or that are 'overdue'

- Record the bills you receive and view bills that are paid, due for payment or overdue

- Check how much you owe your suppliers and, more important, find out how much you are owed by your customers

- Check the account status of your customers and suppliers. For example, you will be able to see at a glance which accounts are over the credit limit, inactive or on-hold

- View and keep track of any recurring entries you have set up in Sage 50

- Quickly check the status of invoices, sales orders and purchase orders. For example, you may want to see which invoices or credit notes are due for printing or which have yet to be posted

- Keep track of your stock levels. You can easily and quickly check for out of stock items, items which are below re-order level, on order or which have been allocated

Hot tip

If you need to clear all your To Do entries in one go simply click on Clear To Do Entries from the Settings menu.

Don't forget

Use the Contacts option to check the people you need to speak to, or have spoken with recently, plus any overdue calls that need to be made. This information is linked directly to the customer and supplier record Contacts tab and will automatically update the relevant future, today, overdue and completed contacts folder.

The Task Manager Desktop

Your Sage 50 Task Manager desktop features a menu bar, a stacked toolbar, an application toolbar and a split screen, with tree view on the left and list view on the right.

From the desktop you can set up tasks, remind yourself of jobs to do etc. To bring up the desktop do the following:

 From the Sage 50 menu, click on Tools, then click Task Manager

 The Menu Bar provides a list of options using drop-down menus

 This is the stacked toolbar area

 This is the List View area

Click on Tasks or Company for the respective toolbars

Select a folder in the Tree View area to bring up a list

You can resize the View areas if required

175

Don't forget

The Application toolbar offers different options with different functions, depending upon the Tasks chosen from the Stacked toolbar.

Hot tip

Options available from the Application toolbar are also available from the Tasks menu, including New, Open, Delete, Pay and Properties.

Hot tip

Use the List View screen (right hand side of the screen) as a shortcut to your tasks, transactions, bills, recurring entries etc. by double-clicking on the required entry.

Setting Up a To Do Task

Use the To Do option to create a list of tasks you need to complete. The type of tasks include a General Reminder, Send overdue letters, Print management reports, etc. Any additional information that may prove useful can be entered within the Description and Notes boxes.

Once saved, the task appears in the Current Tasks folder on the To Do list. This list can then be viewed at any time. To set up a To Do task, proceed as follows:

176

1 From the Task Manager, click on the To Do option from the Tasks stacked toolbar

2 Click New from the application toolbar

3 Select the reminder type from the drop down list box

To Do Entry			
Details			
Type	General Reminder		
Date Due	11/10/2008		
Description			☐ Task Complete
Delegate To	MANAGER		
Notes			
			OK Cancel

4 Enter date when task is due for completion, plus a suitable Description, e.g. chase overdue payments

5 Type any special instructions in the Notes area

6 Click OK to save

Recording a New Bill

The Bills option provides a useful and convenient way of recording all your bills, such as rates, rent, etc. Once the payment information is entered and saved, the bill will appear in the Current Bills folder on the Bills list. These details can be edited if required at this stage.

Use the Task Manager then to quickly view which bills are paid, due or overdue. To record a new bill:

1 Using Task Manager, click on the Bills option from the Tasks stacked toolbar

2 Click New from the File menu

3 Enter the nominal code for the bill to, e.g. if paying your telephone bill the default nominal ledger account is 7502

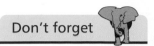

Don't forget

When the bill details are saved, it will appear in the Current Bills folder on the Bills list. If required you can then edit your bill details.

Hot tip

References entered into the Ref box will appear in the Audit Trail for cross referencing.

177

Bill Record ☒

Nominal/Category Details

Pay To 7502 ▾   Telephone

Details

Details [   ]   Ref [   ]

Net 0.00   Tax Code T 1 17.50 ▾   Vat 0.00

Bill date 11/10/2008   Due date 11/10/2008

Payment Details

Amount 0.00   Date paid / /   Outstanding 0.00

[OK]   [Cancel]

4 Enter a Transaction description, then Net amount of bill

5 Enter the date bill was received

6 Enter the date bill is due to be paid

7 Check all details are correct and click OK to save

Don't forget

If a bill is not paid by the Due Date, the task is moved to the Overdue Bills folder.

Paying a Bill

Use the Pay option to quickly and easily pay any current or outstanding bills which have been previously set up using Task Manager. To action bill payment the only detail required is the Bank Account nominal code you want to pay the bill from, as shown here:

1 Select Bills from the Tasks stacked toolbar

2 Select either Current Bills or Overdue Bills folder from the Tree view

3 Select the bill required from the List View

4 Click the Pay option from the application toolbar

178

Bill Payment

Bank Account

Bank 1200 ▢ Bank Current Account

Payment Details

Ref 100394 Date 31/08/2008 ▦

Net 235.00 ▦ Tax Code T 1 17.50 ▢ Vat 41.13 ▦

[OK]   [Cancel]

5 Enter nominal code of Bank account to pay the bill from and click OK to pay the bill

6 The bill is now paid and moves into the Paid Bills folder

7 Click on Paid Bills folder & double-click on the bill you have just paid

8 Note Record now shows payment details

Bill Record

Nominal/Category Details

Pay To 5910 ▢ Hire Purchase

Details

Details Van Hire Ref 100394

Net 235.00 ▦ Tax Code T 1 17.50 ▢ Vat 41.13 ▦

Bill date 15/08/2008 ▦ Due date 31/08/2008 ▦

Payment Details

Amount 276.13 ▦ Date paid 31/08/2008 ▦ Outstanding 0.00 ▦

[OK]   [Cancel]

9 Click OK to close

Accounts Due

Use the Accounts Due option from the Tasks stack to identify who owes you money, i.e. Sales Overdue, Sales Due and Sales Within Settlement. You can also check who you owe money to by viewing the Purchases Overdue, Purchases Due and Purchases Within Settlement folders.

To find out which customers owe you money

1 From the Tasks stacked toolbar, select Accounts Due and click the Sales Overdue folder

2 Note transaction list of overdue payments

3 For more details, select a transaction

4 Click Properties from the application toolbar

5 The Transaction Details window appears

Transaction Details

Account Details

A/C	PAT001	Name	Patterson & Graham Garages
No.	1224	Contact	Simon Billington
		Telephone	0987 678 234

Values

Net	902.50
Tax	153.99
Paid	0.00
	1056.49

Transaction Details

| Type | Sales Invoice | Ref | 76 |
| Details | JP030 Jet Printer | Date | 05/08/2008 |

First Previous Next Last   OK

6 Use these buttons to move between different transactions in the list

7 When finished click OK

Hot tip

Use the Phone button to automatically dial your customer telephone number. Your computer (with modem) needs to share the same line as your telephone.

Hot tip

To view details of different transactions on the list, make full use of the First, Previous, Next or Last buttons.

Don't forget

For a printout of debtors refer to the Customers Reports window.

Account Status

The Account Status option lets you view accounts that match certain criteria. For example, Sales Over Credit Limit, Sales On Hold, Purchase Over Credit Limit or Purchase On Hold. If you require more detailed information about a transaction, select it and click the Properties button from the application toolbar.

1. From the Sage 50 Task Manager window, choose the Account Status option from the Tasks stacked toolbar

2. Select the folder you require from the Tree View list

3. Highlight the required account from the List view

4. Click the Properties button on the toolbar

Hot tip

You can quickly print out a list of customers On Hold or customers Over Credit Limit from the Sage 50 Customers, Reports window.

A/C	Name	Balance
BBS001	Bobs Building Supplies	4309.77
BUS001	Business Exhibitions	6603.30
FGL001	F G Landscape & Design	11260.26
GRA001	Graham Electonics	4149.09
KIN001	Kinghorn & French	7398.35
MAC001	Macolm Hall Associates	6927.16
MIB001	Mikes Insurance Services	3597.16
MIL001	Mile Road Health Centre	5644.12
PAT001	Patterson & Graham Garages	1971.73
SDE001	S D Enterprises	5939.68
SHO001	The Show Lodge	7148.07
VID001	The Video Rental Company	2041.66

Sage Task Manager — File, Tasks, Settings, Help — New, Open, Delete, Pay, Properties. Tasks: To Do, Contacts, Bills, Accounts Due, Account Status, Company. Account Status folders: Sales Over Cre, Sales On Hold, Sales Inactive, Sales Credit Cl, Sales Beyond, Purchase Ove, Purchase On H, Purchase Inac, Purchase Bey.

11/10/2008

Hot tip

In the Account Details window use the First, Previous, Next and Last buttons to move between different account transactions.

5. When finished, click OK to exit

Account Details

Account Details
A/C SHO001 Name The Show Lodge
Contact Lesley Walton
Telephone 0121 383 0345

Aged Analysis

Future	Current	Period 1	Period 2	Period 3	Older
0.00	0.00	4151.77	2996.30	0.00	0.00

First Previous Next Last OK

The Recurring Option

Using the Task Manager you can view any recurring entries you have set for various transaction types, namely Receipt, Payment, Journal Debit or Journal Credit.

You can view further details on the transactions, but you cannot change these details. To view details on a recurring payment you set up in Sage 50, do the following:

1 From the Sage 50 Task Manager window, choose the Recurring option from the Tasks stacked toolbar

2 Select the folder you require from the Tree View list, e.g. Payments

3 Highlight the required payment from the List view

4 Click the Properties button on the application toolbar

5 The details appear for the selected recurring entry

Hot tip

To set up your recurring entries simply select the Recurring option from the Bank toolbar. Refer to chapter 5, page 67, for more information about setting up recurring entries.

Hot tip

For detailed information about a recurring entry, select the transaction and choose the Properties option from the application toolbar.

Recurring Entry Properties

Transaction Type	Bank Payment

Recurring Entry From/To

Bank A/C From	1200	Bank Current Account
Nominal Code	7200	Electricity

Recurring Entry Details

Transaction Ref	DD/STO	Details	Electrcity Direct Debit
Department	0 - ** Not Applicable **		

Posting Frequency

Every	4	Total Reqd. Postings	0
Start Date	01/09/2006	Finish Date	Perpetual
Last Posted	01/09/2008	Suspend Posting	☐

Posting Amounts

Net Amount	150.00	Tax Code	T3 -0.00	VAT 12.00

Close

Beware

Remember you cannot change the recurring entry details from within the Task Manager.

6 Click Close when finished

Stock Option

The Task Manager is a handy way of keeping track of your stock. It provides you with a fast and efficient way of seeing what is out of stock, below the reorder level, on order and allocated.

By using Task Manager for regular monitoring of stock you can make decisions about items which need re-ordering or stock you are waiting for.

1 Select the Stock option from the Tasks stacked toolbar

2 Select the folder required in the Tree View

Code	Description	Qty Stock	Reorder Level
BOARD001	Whiteboard - Drywipe (900 x 1200)	-5.00	1.0
BOOKS002	A4 Carbon Copy Book - Triplicate	-4.00	20.0
BOOKS003	Shorthand Notebook - 80 Sheets	64.00	100.0
CAS001	AT Mini Tower Case	9.00	10.0
CAS002	ATX Mini Tower Case	6.00	10.0
CAS003	ATX Desktop Case	1.00	10.0
CDR001	CDR08432 Read/Write CD Drive	-3.00	5.0
CDR002	CDR10432 Read/Write DVD Drive	1.00	5.0
CDR003	CDR12432 Read/Write CD Drive	2.00	5.0
DISK002	Disk - CDR (640MB)	6.00	30.0
ENV004	Envelope - Brown (110 x 220) Window	12.00	15.0
FLIP002	Flip Chart - A1 Pad (Recycled)	8.00	10.0
LABELS001	A4 Labels (68x99) - Inkjet	3.00	10.0
MEM002	DIMM 512mb 500Mhz	9.00	10.0
MEM003	DIMM 128mb 100Mhz	9.00	10.0
MON001	15" Monitor	4.00	10.0
MOTH001	MTH1000 Motherboard	10.00	10.0
MOTH002	MTH2000 Motherboard	8.00	10.0

11/10/2008

3 Relevant details appear in the list area for your information

4 Use the scroll bars to view all the available details

Invoices Option

Within Task Manager you can view the status of any invoices or credit notes that you have recorded.

Invoices and credit notes are listed separately depending on whether they have been printed or posted. You can also quickly view which invoices or credit notes need to be printed or posted.

For example, do the following to quickly view a list of invoices which have not yet been posted:

1 From the Task Manager window, click on the down button on the Tasks stacked toolbar until Invoices appears

2 Click on the Invoices option

	No.	Date	Name	Amount
	77	13/08/2008	Business Exhibitions	146.94
	78	13/08/2008	Kinghorn & French	52.68
	81	18/08/2008	Swan Leisure Centre	56.72
	83	19/08/2008	John Smith Studios	55.81
	84	22/08/2008	Mikes Insurance Services	71.91
	85	22/08/2008	County Golf Supplies	444.84
	86	13/09/2008	Business Exhibitions	189.03
	87	13/08/2008	S D Enterprises	1797.75
	88	11/09/2008	Business Exhibitions	146.94
	89	13/09/2008	Bronson Inc	0.00
	90	15/09/2008	Palmer Energy Ltd	0.00
	91	11/10/2008	County Golf Supplies	278.02

Sage Task Manager — File Tasks Settings Help — New Open Delete Pay Properties — Tasks — Invoices — Inv to Print / Inv to Post / Crd to Print / Crd to Post — Recurring — Stock — Invoices — SOP — POP — Company — 11/10/2008

3 Select Inv to Post folder

4 A list of all invoices not yet posted appears

Sales Order Processing

From Task Manager you can view the status of your Sales Orders directly. A selection of folders is available for you to view the type of sales orders required. For example, orders that are 'To Allocate', 'Cancelled', 'Held', etc.

It is important to remember, however, that you can only view the details in this screen. If you need to create a new Sales Order or make any changes, you will have to return to the SOP option in Sage 50.

As an example, if you wanted a list of allocated Sales Orders not yet delivered, you could use the SOP Reports facility to print out a suitable report, or you can do a quick view from the Task Manager as follows:

Hot tip

You can also access Sales Orders by selecting Tasks from the Task Manager menu and clicking on Sales Orders.

1 From Task Manager, click the SOP option on the Tasks Stacked toolbar

2 Select the Allocated, to Despatch folder

Don't forget

You will need to return to the SOP option in the Sage 50 to perform any sales order functions.

No.	Date	Name	Amount
28	13/08/2008	Bobs Building Supplies	328.35
32	31/08/2008	S D Enterprises	1586.25
33	31/08/2008	Palmer Energy Ltd	2669.03
34	11/10/2008	Bobs Building Supplies	328.35

3 A list of Completed Sales Orders appears in the View area

Purchase Order Processing

Just as with Sales Orders, use the Task Manager to quickly display the status of your Purchase Orders when you do not need a printed copy. Options available are To Order and To Deliver.

For example, to view a list of Purchase Orders that are 'To Deliver' follow these simple steps:

1 From the Task Manager window, choose the POP option from the Tasks stacked toolbar (you may have to use the down button on the stacked toolbar to bring it into view)

2 Select the To Deliver folder in the Tree View

3 A list of Purchase Orders To Deliver appears in the View area

The Company Stack

This feature is useful for quickly viewing your Company Details, such as Name, Address, Telephone, Fax, VAT Reg. number, Web Site and e-Mail.

These details, however, cannot be edited using this screen. To do so you will need to exit from the Task Manager and return to Sage 50 toolbar. Then, select Company Preferences from the Sage 50 Settings menu and make your changes using the Address tab (see page 11).

To quickly view Company Details from the Task Manager just do the following:

1 Click on the Company button at the foot of the stacked toolbar

2 Click on Company Details to view information

Hot tip

You can also select Company Details from the Settings menu on the Sage 50 Task Manager toolbar to view or amend any of your Company Details.

3 The Details window appears, click OK when finished

Index

H

I

J

L

M

N

U

V

W

Y